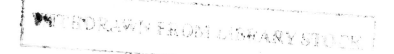

French
Decorative
Art

1900-1942

Yvonne Brunhammer and Suzanne Tise

French Decorative Art

THE SOCIETE DES ARTISTES DECORATEURS

1900-1942

With the participation of Jean-Pierre Khalifa
and the Société des artistes décorateurs

Flammarion

Flammarion, 26, rue Racine, 75006 Paris

Notice

The texts of the introductions, written by Yvonne Brunhammer, were
translated from the French by Jean-Marie Clarke.

The dates of the works illustrated correspond to the year that they were
shown at the Salons.

The translation of this book was assisted by a grant from the French Ministry
of Culture and Communication.

ISBN 2-08-013505-8

Design by François Abegg
Index and photo research by Catherine Diéval-Dupouy
Typeset by Photocomposition Franc-Comtoise, Dole.
Photoengraving by Bussière Arts Graphiques, Paris
Printed in France by Imprimerie Clerc, Saint-Amand-Montrond
Bound by Relieure Brun, Malesherbes.

Contents

Preface

We began our research on the history of the Société des artistes décorateurs simply in order to reconstruct our archives, but the discoveries were so rich that we decided to tell our history in a book for which Yvonne Brunhammer, curator at the musée des Arts décoratifs, and Suzanne Tise, art historian, have accepted to write the text.

The Société des artistes décorateurs was born with the twentieth century, and participated in the principal events that marked French artistic life since 1901: the end of Impressionism and the artistic revolutions of the first decade of the twentieth century, and the Universal Expositions held in France and abroad. The Société survived two world wars, economic crises, and changes in governments; it was present as industry entered everyday life, and helped to introduce many new techniques and materials into interior design.

Its thirty-one Salons demonstrate the vitality of artistic creation during a period when materials and techniques evolved with a rapidity previously unknown.

By telling the history of the Société des artistes décorateurs we hope to contribute a new chapter to the history of art and the *art de vivre* of France.

Jean-Pierre Khalifa
President of the Société des artistes décorateurs

Foreword

Founded in the aftermath of the Universal Exposition of 1900, the Société des artistes décorateurs was a professional association of architects, artisans, and designers—the first to emerge after the abolition of the corporations in 1791. In a cosmopolitan Europe that no longer considered the Parisian model the unique paradigm of elegance, it attempted to promote modernity in the decorative arts and to maintain Paris as the world centre of the luxury industries. From the beginning, it tried to diffuse a typically French savoir-faire throughout the nation and abroad by organizing an annual salon. The only independant salon reserved for the decorative arts, considered until then as "minor arts", this important annual event allows us to follow the evolution of the decorative arts in France through the work of the best artists of the period.

During the first forty years of the Société's existence, nearly two thousand artists became members, and many more were invited to participate in its salons. Faced with the impossibility of discussing the work of so many artists, we have presented only their contributions to the salons and traced the history of the Société itself, its confrontation with industry, its search for modernity, and its struggle to defend the professional interests of a corporation.

The archives of the Société des artistes décorateurs are incomplete and dispersed. We were able to reconstruct its history through the minutes of its committee meetings, furnished by Jean-Pierre Khalifa, current president of the Société, through the bulletins published irregularly between 1901 and 1939, and through the salon catalogues and articles in contemporary reviews—the only witnesses to the ephemeral ensembles created for each salon.

We have supplemented this documentation with illustrations of works housed in museums and private collections.

Yvonne Brunhammer and Suzanne Tise

1. *Manuel Orazi,* Poster for
La Maison Moderne, *c. 1900.*
Paris, musée de la Publicité.

1900-1914

Until the late eighteenth century, French designers and craftsmen had always laboured within the narrow confines of a corporation, producing highly specialized work under close supervision. When corporations were abolished in 1791, both artisans and manufacturers were thrust into new social and economic realities. The new stakes were clear for the Minister of the Interior under the Directory, François de Neufchâteau, when he organized the *Public Exhibition of the Products of French Industry*, to bring the various crafts under the wing of industry and make industrial products known to the public.

The exhibition opened in the autumn of 1798 on the Champ de Mars under arcades designed by the painter David. It assembled 110 exhibitors: clothmakers, hatmakers, gunsmiths, mechanics, founders, engravers, and printers, as well as manufacturers of ceramics, porcelain, crystal and wallpaper. It was with this exhibition that the *useful arts*—rather than the *liberal arts*—became a national priority and remained so throughout the nineteenth century. Jean Chaptal, a renowned chemist and Minister of the Interior under Napoléon, proposed to the First Consul that an exhibition of French industrial products become an annual event that would be part of the festivities commemorating the foundation of the Republic. The first exhibition under the Consulat was held in 1801 in the courtyard of the palais des Sciences et des Arts (today known as the Louvre), just a few steps from the Salon Carré, which had given its name to the famous *Salons* of painting and sculpture. During the eighteenth century, these Salons were reserved for painters, sculptors, and engravers of the French Academy, and excluded craftsmen and industrialists who engaged in commerce, an activity forbidden to Academy members. Nevertheless, this physical proximity foretold an alliance that would be realized in the Paris Universal Expositions that began in 1855.

These industrial exhibitions took place irregularly during the first half of the nineteenth century, buffeted by the vicissitudes of an unstable political and economic climate. The intention of its promoters, however, did not waver, and the use of the term *products* for both ordinary and luxury objects was an indication of the government's desire to help craftsmen assimilate the new advances in science and technology. But the dream of a union between art and industry, which would continue to fuel the cause of the *useful arts*, was broken by the inability to provide machines with models adapted to their possibilities. Neither artisans nor the public could imagine the leap into an industrial logic that required a complete redefinition of the art product.

Thus began the vicious circle of copies and pastiches, which were given the optimistic label of *eclecticism* to mask their lack of imagination. Though some of these styles were not devoid of charm, the small industrial production of everyday and luxury objects between

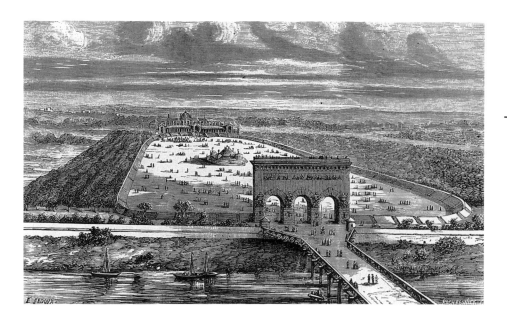

2. Exposition publique des produits de l'industrie française, 1798. Engraving. Paris, bibliothèque historique de la Ville de Paris.

the July monarchy and the salutary breakthrough of Art Nouveau showed that the initial dream had failed.

During the last decades of the nineteenth century, the involvement of artists, painters, sculptors and engravers in the vogue for orientalism and *japonisme* fostered a demand for a new kind of decorative arts: handmade, one-of-a-kind pieces, not the mass production of usually tasteless period copies. The decline of the 1900 style at the turn of the century was partly caused by the industrial production of banal hybrid versions of (the otherwise inventive) Art Nouveau.

The Société des artistes décorateurs was founded in 1901 at the crossroads of arts, crafts, and industry. From the beginning, however, it suffered the same contradictions that had troubled French decorative arts since the end of the eighteenth century. During the first decade of the twentieth century, when profound changes were taking place in the social, scientific and cultural concepts of time and space, the young Société could not keep up with the times. It was unable to assimilate the scientific and aesthetic revolutions of the first decade of the century: Einstein's Theory of Relativity, the discovery of new properties of matter by Pierre and Marie Curie, and the questioning of the pictorial representation of space by the Cubist painters. Most important, it was hindered by the same attitudes that had led to the demise of Art Nouveau. And even if its goals were sometimes clouded by the pervasive belief that the artist was a creator of models and patterns, the Société's founders emphasized the relationship between designers and industrialists, striving to create a group synergy rather than favour individuals. With the belief that industry could respond to art's social aims, as early as 1911 it planned an International Exhibition of Decorative Arts to be held in Paris in 1925, a project which coincided with the rise of such socialist groups as the SFIO (Section française de l'internationale ouvrière) and the CGT (Confédération générale du travail).

And yet, while planning its very first Salon at the Petit Palais in 1904, the Société adopted a position that it would rarely abandon: rather than presenting the more ordinary Restaurant Room suggested by the sculptor Rupert Carabin, it decided to present an elegant Tea-room and thereby gave its blessing to the luxury industries.

It was the Salon d'Automne of 1912, and not the Salon des artistes décorateurs, that offered the first group exhibit representing the new epoch: the *Maison Cubiste* designed by various painters, sculptors and decorators assembled around André Mare and Raymond Duchamp-Villon.

Yvonne Brunhammer

3. Raymond Duchamp-Villon, Model for the Maison cubiste, Salon d'Automne, 1910.

4. André Mare, "Bourgeois Interior" for the Maison Cubiste, Salon d'Automne, 1910.

The *Société des artistes décorateurs* was founded in Paris on February 7th, 1901 by René Guilleré (1877-1932), a lawyer representing the Association des sculpteurs-modeleurs, along with fourteen other artists and designers including Eugène Belville, Jules Brateau, Rupert Carabin and Louis Carrier-Belleuse.[1] Extremely heterogeneous in its make-up, and with an annual membership of approximately 250 during the first forty years of its existence, the Société never officially espoused a specific style or aesthetic theory, but devoted itself to protecting the rights of designers and to elevating their professional status to that enjoyed by fine artists.[2] Conforming to the newly-created Loi des Associations of 1901, it was a non-profit organization, and according to the Société's first published statement, its initial ambitions were simple: to "unite the members of all of the corporations of designers and craftsmen in order to defend their material interests, and to foster special exhibitions of decorative ensembles".[3]

In many ways, the new Société was the product of the nineteenth-century decorative arts reform movement that had preoccupied artistic and government leaders in France for more than fifty years. But the immediate catalyst for its foundation was the German decorative arts display at the Paris Universal Exposition of 1900. Participating in this exhibit were leading artists from the Munich Jugendstil movement, many of whom were involved in the Vereinigte Werkstätten für Kunst im Handwerk (United Workshops for Art in Handicraft), a powerful association founded in 1897 to produce and market designs by Jugendstil artists. In contrast to the practice in most French pavilions, where furnishings were either showcased individually as single masterpieces or as a collection of disparate objects, the Germans had built entire interiors

5. Private interior in Paris, c. 1900.

within their pavilion, designed and decorated by a single artist or a group of artists working in collaboration.[4] They astonished the French public by the conceptual unity of their ensembles and the originality and modernity of their work.[5] René Guilleré was one of many in France to realize that the success of the German presentation in 1900 was due to the organization of the artists into professional groups like the Werkstätten. This group provided a threefold service: it established a forum through which artists could find craftsmen to execute their designs, it created special exhibitions for craftsmen and manufacturers, and consequently it made modern decorative arts known to prospective purchasers and connoisseurs.[6] While French reformers had been calling for a similar union between art and industry for more than half a century, nothing like the Werkstätten existed in France. For the most part French designers worked individually and they disposed of no institutional structure for exhibiting or promoting their designs. Guilleré was convinced that because of this lack of professional organization the decorative arts in France were in crisis, and would eventually succumb to foreign competition if measures were not taken to support them.

This crisis stemmed from several sources. The abolition of corporations in 1791 by the Revolutionary Le Chapelier Law meant the end of the institutions that had upheld high standards of quality through a long and thorough training of apprentices. Commercial capitalism was gradually restructuring the social and material aspects of handicraft manufacturing and, having no protection through professional organizations or from the state, artisans were at the mercy of their employers. Apprentices were often treated as little more than domestic

6. Study, c. 1903. Chimney by
Raymond Bigot and Eugène Gaillard;
mural paintings by Joseph-Marius Avy;
stained glass by Félix Gaudin;
desk by Edouard Colonna;
chairs by Eugène Gaillard.

Right page:

7. Guillaume Dubufe's Studio,
43 avenue de Villiers, Paris.

8. Salon of the Société nationale
des beaux-arts, c. 1894,
decoration by Guillaume Dubufe.

Following double page:

9. Paul Follot, Tea service, 1903 (1904 Salon).
Silver. Paris, musée d'Orsay.

workers, and with the arrival of mechanization and the division of labour, the time and materials needed to train them properly seemed an unnecessary expenditure. Decorative artists were also without protection. They were not usually allowed to sign the designs that they provided for manufacturers, and they had no legal recourse (even if they could have afforded it) against their designs being copied. Artists involved in the decorative arts, moreover, unlike their colleagues in the fine arts, had no salon devoted specifically to their work. The Société nationale des beaux-arts opened its doors to them in 1891, but the decorative arts were still considered minor arts and were relegated to a secondary position within the Salon.

The most pressing problems facing French art industries however were historicism and eclecticism. Many Parisian decorative arts industries were based on the production of copies or pastiches of past French styles which had been enormously successful on the export market throughout the nineteenth century. But during the 1880s countries like Germany, Spain and Italy, where labour could be thirty

per cent cheaper than in Paris, began producing copies of French styles that were passed off as French craftsmanship to inexperienced buyers, thus causing the French production to lose its uniqueness.[7] To remedy this, artists and decorative arts reformers began calling for a modern and specifically French style, eventually creating the Art Nouveau movement of the 1890s. They had hoped that the new style, whose structural logic and ornamentation were inspired by an intense study of nature rather than historical styles (although in fact, it was not devoid of references to the French rococo), would be a new departure for the decorative arts in France, but the style was attacked by critics at the Exposition of 1900, and was apparently a commercial failure with the general public.[8] By the time the Société was founded in 1901, even the most ardent supporters of the Art Nouveau movement like Frantz Jourdain (architect of La Samaritaine department store), began to criticize the unbridled fantasy of its botanical forms and its symbolist references as an elitist art that appealed only to dilettantes and neurotic aesthetes:

It is high time we abolished the symbolist theories, those unwholesome dreams, conventional types, women without sex, androgynous men, all the inept nonsense with which they have tried to becloud the clarity of the French genius! . . . We have not escaped the Roman chariots only to ensconce ourselves in nightmarish ivory towers![9]

As Guilleré explained when he developed the first project for a Society of Decorative Artists in 1900 (published under the title Projet d'une Société nationale des arts décoratifs), the creation of modern furnishings should not be considered only in terms of style and ornament; rather, attention should be drawn to the relationship between the artist, the object and the public. Pointing to the failure of the Art Nouveau movement to provide a modern style of domestic furnishings that answered the needs of a broad sector of society, he asked:

> Does it [Art Nouveau] think that it has answered, as it promised to do, the new needs of our time by filling its works with amorphous forms, unreal nudes and unnatural studies of nature? Have its colours, its lines and its forms risen above the confusion of a rough sketch and attained an artistic unity? What has it produced? A few artistic successes, some "unique pieces" which we have enclosed in our museums or display-cases. But has it driven out the pastiches and copies of old styles, or the dismal bourgeois luxury of the Henri II sideboard? No, and the results obtained are insufficient considering the effort expended.[10]

Guilleré was confident that a professional society of decorative artists, similar to the Société des artistes français, for example, would provide an opportunity for exchange and cooperation among decorative artists, artisans and manufacturers. It would encourage the creation of a modern style, educate consumers through exhibitions of modern decorative arts, and make the government aware of the need to support the decorative arts through subsidies and commissions.[11] He believed that in a modern society the decorative arts were the most democratic and that it was the duty of the state to encourage artists in their mission to beautify the home, the street and the city:

> Luxury in a democracy must no longer hide in pictures and statues in a gallery, it must show itself in the broad light of day, on the façades of houses, embellishing the streets and public squares. Was this not the ideal of the Greek people, and the

same ideal which Viollet-le-Duc proposed for our democracy? And to recall the thoughts of the Count de Laborde, art takes on a real importance and a true nobility when it responds to 'social needs'.[12]

1900-1914

The first general assembly of the Société des artistes décorateurs took place on May 24th, 1901, in the meeting room of *Le Journal*, rue de la Grange Batellière, under the presidency of Louis Carrier-Belleuse, and the first elections for a governing body were held. The decorative painter Guillaume Dubufe was elected president; vice-presidents were Louis Carrier-Belleuse and Jules Brateau; secretaries, Eugène Belville and Griffrath; and treasurer, decorative artist Edme Couty. Altogether, the original committee was composed of thirty-three members, including some well-known artists of the Art Nouveau movement: the sculptor and furniture-maker Rupert Carabin; the ceramist Albert Dammouse; graphic artist and professor Eugène Grasset; the leader of the Nancy School, Victor Prouvé; the sculptor Pierre Roche and the architect Henri Sauvage.[13]

Although Dubufe (1853-1909) did not have a reputation as one of the most advanced artists of his time, he was a good choice as president of the Société. Member of the Société des artistes français, president of the Société des aquarellistes, Dubufe was a well-known portraitist and decorative painter who had received numerous official commissions: he had decorated the ceilings for the Comédie-Française (1883), the Salle des Fêtes of the Elysée (1889) and the Bibliothèque of the Sorbonne (1897).[14] Aside from having extensive professional and social relations useful to the new Société in its campaign for government and private sponsorship, he had directed the innovative installations of artwork in the Palais des beaux-arts for the first salon of the Société nationale des beaux-arts in 1890. This new exhibition society, of which Dubufe had been a founding member, was the first to include decorative arts in an official salon.[15] Dubufe had also engineered an im-portant event at the salon of the Société nationale in 1896. Usually the decorative arts were displayed individually rather than in ensembles that reproduced the atmosphere of a domestic interior. Dubufe developed from his own designs for a Salon/Library the first full-scale project that called upon the collaboration of a broad range of members. The ensemble intended to demonstrate the principle of the unity of the arts.[16]

The Société accomplished some of its most important work during the first two years of its existence. It devoted itself to several pressing issues concerning the decorative arts and the status of decorative artists, and even hired a law firm to study the relationship between artists and industrialists and to offer legal counsel to its members. In 1902 the group petitioned the Prefet de la Seine to include a greater number of decorative artists on the juries for the annual *Concours des ouvriers d'art*, a competition that could award a reduction in military service to the best young artisans to permit them to pursue their training.[17] That same year they influenced the decision of the Minister of Commerce to modify the law of July 1793 on artistic property, to allow decorative artists to benefit from the same protection as painters and sculptors.[18]

The Société also began to develop a working policy to cooperate with industry for the execution and diffusion of the artists' designs. This was particularly important because the lack of guidelines or legislation had created constant discord between artists and manufacturers. The Société produced a contract that would be signed by the artist, the manufacturer and the Société, which would protect both the designer and the manufacturer, and permit the Société to control standards of quality. An object created through such an arrangement would then be

10. *Henri Sauvage and Charles Sarazin,*
The Dressing Room of an Actress, *1904.*

sold by the sales office of the Société with the special stamp, "Edition de la Société des artistes décorateurs".[19] Although collaboration with industry was perceived by more progressive members as fundamental to the life of the association and to the modernization of the decorative arts, it was a source of dissent within the group, because certain members, fearing an excessive commercialization of the association, were ambivalent about allowing artists to exhibit models that they had not executed themselves. After lengthy discussion among members of the governing committee, it was determined that, realistically, only creators of small *objets d'art* were capable of entirely conceiving and executing a work of decorative art, and that although the Société should remain a society of *artistes créateurs de modèles*, a certain amount of cooperation with industry was essential. In an eventual exhibition, however, work created in cooperation with manufacturers would be exhibited under the name of the artist, with the manufacturer's name listed second, and the works were still treated as fine art rather than commercial products—artists were not permitted to put their addresses or the prices of their works on their stands in the Salon.[20]

From the beginning, one of the main goals of the Société was to exhibit unified decorative ensembles that would call upon the participation of as many branches of the arts as possible. But the first committee discussions on the nature of the planned ensembles revealed the persistent disagreement among the members about what constituted an original work of art, and the definition and role of the *artiste décorateur*. What would be the exact nature of their collaboration with industry and commerce?[21] Were they to consider themselves fine artists, or would they allow their aesthetic decisions to be determined by questions of economy and utility? These were vital issues for the Société while it was

planning its first Salon during December 1901.

Rupert Carabin proposed that the theme of the Société's first Salon be the dining-room of a restaurant. This, according to him, was an appropriate solution to the group's needs: it would attract a wide variety of crafts, it could actually be used as a buffet during the exhibition, and it might be sold afterwards to an entrepreneur planning to open a restaurant. Brateau agreed with Carabin, and suggested that the artists make the installation as simple and inexpensive as possible, while maintaining high standards of quality. Griffrath argued, however, that such a theme was too commercial and that it would be wiser and more respectable to petition the state for a commission for a reception room for a ministry.[2] A compromise was finally reached: a Tea-room that would be presented as a corporative *œuvre* of the Société, but aimed at a more elite public than that imagined for Carabin's restaurant. As the committee later explained to its members: "The special public that frequents tea-rooms, an exclusively luxurious and elegant public, would be more amenable to the effects of taste and art than the distracted public of a café."[3] This choice was decisive for the Société. It set the precedent for its future salons and affirmed the Société's chosen role of *artistes-créateurs* who would perpetuate French traditions of elegance and fine craftsmanship.[4] However, an open competition for the Tea-room that was announced in the May 1902 issue of *Art et Décoration* was dropped in 1903, and the reason was never explained in the records of the committee meetings.[5] The first Salon opened in January 1904 at the Petit Palais, with only one collaborative ensemble: the *Loge d'une actrice* (The Dressing-room of an Actress), under the direction of the architects Henri Sauvage and Charles Sarazin, with

contributions by thirty-five members. The Salon was divided into four sections: ensembles, individual objects, a section of "rustic" art by artisans from the French provinces, and a small section devoted to techniques.[6] This sectioning remained in effect until 1907 when the Salon was transferred to the Paris Museum of Decorative Arts under the auspices of the Union centrale des arts décoratifs. Only ensembles and individual works were presented thereafter.

In spite of an apparent initial success, between 1906 and 1910 the Société experienced serious administrative and financial difficulties. Many members announced their resignation for reasons never explained in the committee records: membership dropped from 305 members in 1905 to 191 in 1908. Evidently there was disagreement about the establishment of the Société's admission requirements: some felt that too many decorators with commercial attachments were being admitted. Thus, in November 1908 the statutes defining qualification for admission were modified as follows: "The active members are recognized professional decorators, they are personally and normally authors-creators of designs of decorative, industrial or applied art."[7] With these new restrictions and the departure of one-third of its members, the Salons of 1907 and 1908 were less important than those of 1904 and 1906 (there was no Salon in 1905 or 1909), and were scarcely mentioned in the press. At the request of the Comité des expositions à l'étranger, the Société did organize small, but successful, presentations at the international decorative arts expositions held in Milan in 1906, and in Copenhagen in 1909.

The general style of the works presented at the Salons of the Société between 1904 and 1910 was influenced by Art Nouveau. But since 1900 critical

11. Henri-Jules-Ferdinand Bellery-Desfontaines, Table, 1900 (1910 Salon). Walnut. Paris, musée des Arts décoratifs.

12. Mathieu Gallerey, Wardrobe, 1906.

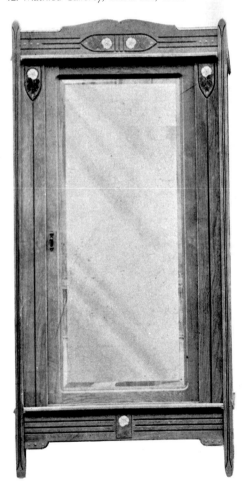

opinion had turned even more strongly against Art Nouveau, and it was repeatedly attacked with invectives like "a fury of ugliness", and a "moral and material failure".[8] Although small decorative objects and graphic art continued to be heavily influenced by the style, designers abandoned the agit-

ated and curvilinear delicacy of pre-1900 Art Nouveau, which required expensive handwork, for fuller and more sober, often rectilinear forms in heavier woods that recalled Belgian Art Nouveau and English Arts and Crafts furnishings. This tendency was encouraged by discussions among decorative arts reformers on the possibility of an *art pour tous* or "art for the people", an idea that had become popular with the rise of socialism and the working-class movement during the 1890s.[29] This is why in its first Salon the Société had turned its attention to "rustic" art from the French provinces: the organizers believed that its simple economical construction and direct use of materials provided an excellent model for artists looking for an alternative to Art Nouveau. The exhibits by Paul Follot in 1904 and Mathieu Gallerey in 1906 were representative of this move towards more simplified furnishings. The oak bedroom ensemble that Gallerey presented in 1906, decorated only with marquetry rosettes, could be largely mechanically produced and was intended to sell for the modest sum of 500 francs.

But this new, simpler style, far from reflecting the modern values that the Société claimed to espouse, seldom went beyond an Arts and Crafts ideal, and seemed little suited to urban apartments. Critics soon began complaining about the style's sterility and about its unsuitability to Parisian tastes: "This art is good for men at the very most, it may be tolerated in the country, but it is not for Paris; the women's judgement is that this Germanic fashion is without appeal: it is kitchen furniture."[30]

A dramatic change in the style of the works exhibited in the salons of the Société came about as the result of a second manifestation of the Munich Werkstätten—their appearance in Paris at the Salon d'Automne in 1910. Since

13. *Paul Follot,* Sideboard, *1904.*

14. Louis Majorelle, Door, 1906. Forged iron and copper.

1900 the growing artistic and commercial success of the Werkstätten had been a cause for alarm in France. There was even more concern after an important applied arts exhibition in Munich in 1908, when the French delegation, which included one of the founders of the Société des artistes décorateurs, Rupert Carabin, returned to report that the German exhibition represented for France an "artistic and commercial Sedan".[31] The delegation later reported to a conference on the decorative arts in Nancy that the long-sought-after modern style had not been born in France, but in Germany:

> The ruling principle that inspires the young German school is to create harmonious ensembles through a collaboration of sculpture, painting and architecture, and the group has endeavoured to realize this first by reforming the aesthetics of the home to make the modern house a combined work of art, a practical construction of simple and dignified beauty. . . . Thanks to the simplicity which they intentionally seek, they have succeeded in creating furniture designs of good quality and irreproachable form that may be executed entirely by machine, so that they are within the reach of modest budgets.[32]

It was after the delegation returned from Munich in 1908 that Frantz Jourdain, founder and president of the Salon d'Automne (which attributed an important place to modern decorative arts in its annual Salons), invited the Munich Werkstätten to exhibit in Paris in 1910.[33] Apprehension about the show, nursed by already-existing antagonisms between France and Ger-

15. *Eugène Feuillâtre, Dragonfly Bowl, 1903 (1904 Salon). Silver, crystal and enamel. Paris, musée d'Orsay.*

16. *Eugène Michel, Vase, 1904. Glass. Paris, Félix Marcilhac collection.*

many, began building up months before it opened. In May 1910, the journal *La Réforme Economique* carried the headlines, "The exhibition of the German artists will do a great injustice to the French decorative arts, and may even strike their death blow!" and in June, the *Gaulois* announced "an impending German invasion".[34] When the Salon opened in October, the Munich group, led by Bruno Paul and Richard Riemerschmid, filled eighteen rooms with the finest products of modern German decorative arts organized on the theme of the "House of an Art Lover". Vaguely inspired by the Biedermeier style, the interiors were not particularly innovative, but they demonstrated a sobriety, unity of design and sophistication that completely surprised the French public. The colour schemes were equally unexpected: bright oranges, cobalt blue and brilliant greens—hues virtually unknown in French decoration. Moreover, each artist had called upon the leading painters and sculptors of the day to complete their interiors with corresponding works of art. The French section, in contrast, was devoted to no particular theme, and the individual ensembles were dominated by the Art Nouveau and Arts and Crafts style furnishings that seemed outmoded in comparison.[35] Although the French critics of the Munich exhibition were

17. *Karl Bertsch, Woman's Bedroom, exhibited by the Munich Werkstätten at the Salon d'Automne, 1910.*

ambivalent about the bold colours employed by the German decorators, they agreed that the exhibit was an important and profitable lesson. Roger Marx, for example, praised the way in which the decoration of each room had been placed under the direction of an architect, whose sense of construction always took precedence over decorative details, as well as the sense of discipline, order and method that was often lacking in the French ensembles.[36]

The Salon made a powerful impression in Paris: it was discussed during a meeting of the City Council, and after 1910, a comparison between French and German decorative arts could be found in the reviews of almost all subsequent Parisian decorative arts salons until 1914.[37] The example of the Munich decorators also inspired French designers to define and create a modern and uniquely French style. A change already could be seen at the Salon of the Société des artistes

décorateurs in the spring of 1911. René Guilleré, who had just been elected president of the Société, announced in the introduction to the catalogue that a modern style was being born, one that now owed nothing to the "the primitive extravagances of Art Nouveau".[38] Indeed, Paul Follot and Maurice Dufrène presented new concepts in interiors: they abandoned the heavy straight-lined furnishings in hard woods for lighter and more graceful designs that relied on the oval and the arabesque, and replaced solid woods with more elegant and exotic ones like citron wood, ebony and rosewood. The interiors were more open and airy, and included fewer of the floral patterns in draperies, carpets, friezes and tapestries that had overpowered interiors only a year earlier.

The creation of a modern French style was all the more urgent in 1911 because of a government-sponsored project for an international exhibition of decorative arts to be held in Paris in

1915. The initial project was developed by René Guilleré and the Société in 1911, and co-signed by representatives of French artistic societies engaged in the decorative arts reform movement.[39] According to Guilleré's report, the exhibition was necessary to preserve national honour, and it could have decisive economic and artistic repercussions. France, he said, was gradually losing its position as the world centre of art and taste as other nations developed their own new and original styles of decorative art for mass production. He cited alarming increases in decorative arts imports and the establishment in Paris of dozens of foreign-owned boutiques selling modern designs. To recapture home and export markets, Guilleré urged an international exhibition of decorative arts in Paris that would include only those works that could be designated as truly "modern"—this would prevent artists and manufacturers from continuing to copy historical models, and encourage the development of a style that re-

flected more contemporary concerns. We shall return to the role of the Société in the preparations for the exhibition, which did not take place until 1925, in a later chapter. For now, let it be said that the anticipation of the exhibition led to a whole series of speculations among artists and critics about the characteristics of a new French style. One of the most influential was the essay, *Le Nouveau Style*, published by the landscape gardener and theorist André Vera (1881-1971) in the January 1912 issue of *L'Art Décoratif*. He called for an art founded on reason, on a logic and unity that was expressed in the great French artistic traditions of the past, and particularly in the style of the seventeenth century. At the same time, he said, it was necessary to abandon historicism once and for all in order to pick up the thread of the French tradition, which had been lost after the Revolution of 1848. He recommended, therefore, that artists look to the last true French style, the Louis-Philippe style, for inspiration:

18. Adalbert Niemeyer, Dining-room, exhibited by the Munich Werkstätten at the Salon d'Automne, 1910.

20. *Clément Mère, Cabinet, 1913. Macassar ebony with mother-of-pearl incrustations. Paris, musée des Arts décoratifs.*

19. *Paul Follot, Oval Boudoir, 1912. Maple marquetry.*

"We are seeking qualities of clarity, order and harmony which were complete in the seventeenth century, and furthermore, we want to reestablish contact with this tradition, which seems to have stopped around 1848."[40] Vera went so far as to specify a decorative vocabulary for the new style—baskets and garlands of flowers would become its distinctive features, just as the torch and bows and arrows had constituted the decorative attributes of seventeenth-century decoration.

Vera's text was important: it laid out the formal characteristics of the nascent Art Deco style, and would provide an ideological base for the work of an entire group of young designers trying to find their way out of the impasse of Art Nouveau towards the mythical new style. But his paradigm of modernity had not rejected tradition, and had little to do with design based on notions of function or fitness of purpose. For him, the modern domestic environment would be imbued with meaning and rich with symbols that reflected a cultural renaissance on a national scale.

Vera's article must have appealed to a number of similar spirits in the Parisian world of decorative arts. The Salons of the Société between 1912 and 1914 were dominated by designs that were clearly influenced by styles and craftsmanship from the French past. Paul Follot's *Oval Boudoir* in maple presented at the 1912 Salon made distinct references to the Louis-Philippe style and to the eighteenth century, as did the sumptuous *Oval Salon* presented by master glass-maker and jeweller René Lalique, reveted in porcelain tiles shot through with veins of platinum executed by the Manufacture nationale de Sèvres. The comfortable armchairs in André Groult's *Petit Salon* were drawn from the Louis-Philippe style and French provincial models, but modernized through the brilliant colour combinations of Fauvist painting and the Ballets Russes. Several models of exquisite cabinetwork were presented by Clement Mère at the Salon of 1913; the geometric forms and smooth surfaces beautifully juxtaposed with lavish inlays in mother-of-pearl announced the techniques of craftsmanship that

would become hallmarks of the Art Deco style of the 1920s. In the bedroom ensemble presented by André Mare at the Salon of 1914, as well, we see the Art Deco style develop in the unusual combination of luxurious materials—maple, palisander, rosewood, amaranth—and the stylized rose that would become one of Arts Deco's characteristic decorative motifs.

On the eve of the First World War the Société's Salon was still relatively conservative, devoted to unique works of art and fine craftsmanship. It was most significant in bringing various artists of different pursuits together. They were intensely individualistic, but united in their rejection of a slavish imitation of past styles. The major artistic events of the pre-war years were played out at the Salon d'Automne, with the exhibition of the Munich designers in 1910, and then in 1912 when a group of artists inspired by the ideas of André Vera, led by André Mare and Duchamp-Villon, scandalized the public with their *Maison cubiste*.

The members of the Société looked at their craft from the point of view of the individual designer rather than as a group. In spite of their call for a modern style, in the face of the rationalist and commercialized design proposed by the Munich decorators and a notion of modernity that revolved around questions of economy and technique, they chose to uphold longstanding traditions of French style and craftsmanship. Of course, the practitioners of the luxury crafts had obvious and understandable reasons for clinging to tradition and *métier*—a whole range of interest groups were threatened by a modern style that celebrated the virtues of simplicity and economy. We shall see how the Société sought to preserve these traditions in anticipation of the Exposition internationale des arts décoratifs of 1925.

Suzanne Tise

1904

21. Eugène Grasset, Catalogue cover
for the First Salon of the artistes décorateurs.

22. Paul Follot, Study.

23. Maurice Dufrène, Study.

January-February, Petit Palais

President: Guillaume Dubufe
Vice-president: Louis Carrier-Belleuse
General Secretary: René Guilleré
Treasurer: Edme Couty

The first Salon of the Société des artistes décorateurs comprised four sections:
1. Ensembles
2. Individual displays
3. Models and Projects
4. Rustic Art and Metal Art

One of the major goals of the Société was to encourage designers and artists to work together to create unified decorative ensembles.[41] At the first Salon, eleven such contributions were presented, although only one, The Dressing Room of an Actress (Loge d'actrice) was truly the kind of collaborative effort that the Société hoped to institutionalize. Thirty-five artists, artisans and decorators, directed by the architects Henri Sauvage and Charles Sarazin, cooperated on this Art Nouveau-style interior intended for Sarah Bernhardt.[42] The actress's every need was taken into account, from personal items like powder boxes, scissors and a shoe horn by sculptor Eugène Lelièvre and a brush and soap boxes by Eugène Michel, to elegant furnishings such as Louis Majorelle's dressing table and a chaise longue by Franck Scheidecker and Majorelle. Sarah Bernhardt herself displayed some small decorative objects that she had sculpted. If most of the exhibits at the Salon included unique and expensive pieces involving complicated handwork, the Société also made room for less-refined decorative arts from the French provinces. As critic Clément-Janin explained in his preface to the Salon catalogue, this display of provincial rusticity was intended to encourage artists towards a greater simplicity in design and truth in materials following the extravagances of the Art Nouveau works that had been highly criticized at the 1900 Exposition universelle:

At a time when designers are looking for new forms, seeking—often with good results—original combinations of line and colour, it seems useful to bring together works of art of a more instinctive nature; in other words, works by country craftsmen. It is here that one finds a genuine appliction of the absolute principle of the decorative arts: a close relation between the form and the use of the object. . . .[43]

1906

November-December, Pavillon de Marsan

Catalogue cover: Maurice Dufrène

President: Emile-Seraphin Vernier
Vice-presidents: Jean-Louis Bremond,
Hector Guimard
General Secretary: René Guilleré
Secretaries: Maurice Dufrène,
André Morisset
Treasurer: Edme Couty

24. Maurice Dufrène, Dining-room.
Planetree wood.

25. Eugène Gaillard, Chair, 1906 Salon.
Sculpted palisander, covered in silk,
"golden rain" pattern.
Paris, musée des Arts décoratifs.

26. Bruno Ducrocq, Salon.

1910

27. *Charles-Pierre Stern,*
Hand mirror. *Silver.*

28. *Paul Follot, Bedroom.*

29. *François Decorchemont, Bowl,
1909, (1910 Salon). Pâte de verre.
Paris, musée d'Orsay.*

February-March, Pavillon de Marsan

Catalogue cover:
Ferdinand Bellery-Desfontaines

By 1910, the Société's financial situation had improved considerably. That year the date of the Salon was changed to February to anticipate the Salon d'Automne. At the same time, the Union centrale des arts décoratifs accorded a new exhibition space within the musée des Arts décoratifs on the rue de Rivoli. The big event of the season, however, was not the Société's Salon, but the exhibition of the Munich Werkstätte at the Salon d'Automne. The direction of the Société was well aware of the progress in modern decorative arts made by the German organisation, and planned to make a concerted effort at the 1910 Salon to foster a modern French style. But the majority of the works at the Salon, in spite of their high technical quality, seemed to be caught in a stylistic impasse still largely dominated by Art Nouveau. This was the case, for example, in the hand mirror by Charles-Pierre Stern, the sideboard by Eugène Gaillard, and the bookcase by Pierre Selmersheim, where the decoration was heavy, sculptural and naturalistic. The bedroom by Paul Follot, however, in red mahogany adorned with a geometric motif in ebony marquetry, took a new direction: the forms were sober, more lightweight, and the decoration less exuberant.

30. Hector Guimard, Plate, 1909,
(1911 Salon). Gilt patinated bronze.
Paris, musée des Arts décoratifs.

31. Léon Jallot, Cabinet, Salon 1911.
Amboyna wood.
Paris, musée des Arts décoratifs.

32. André Methey, Vase, 1911. Stoneware.
Paris, musée des Arts décoratifs.

23 February-26 March, Pavillon de Marsan

President: René Guilleré
Vice Presidents: Paul Mezzara,
Hector Guimard
General Secretary: Geo Lamothe
Secretaries: Maurice Dufrène,
Henry de Waroquier
Treasurer: Paul Follot

Exhibition architect: Théodore Lambert

The controversy surrounding the Munich exhibition at the Salon d'Automne of 1910 had the fortunate effect of drawing public attention to the decorative arts. At the Société's salon of the following year the number of visitors quadrupled and sales doubled.[44] The example of the Munich designers also affected the kind of work shown. The lines of Léon Jallot's *Bureau* were sober and almost classical; the piece was enlivened only by the patterns of the burl wood veneer. The dining-room in mahogany and violet wood presented by Maurice Dufrène was a complete turnaround from the floral decorations of Art Nouveau. It was free of the decorative mouldings and stencilled friezes that had created a sense of decorative unity, but

that often overpowered interiors. In general, designers returned to delicate, exotic woods after several years of relying principally on oak and ash. Small decorative objects, however, and particularly metalwork, from the bronze plate by Hector Guimard to Edgar Brandt's grillwork remained inspired by Art Nouveau.

The discipline and organization displayed by the Munich decorators showed to Société members the importance of greater cooperation from industrialists and public authorities in any attempts to renovate the applied arts. In the salon catalogue of 1911, they published the following appeal for support:

The goal towards which our Society is striving is nothing less than the creation of the French styles of the twentieth century. An endeavour which, alas, has received too little encouragement! Not everyone has yet understood the obvious necessity of having styles that harmonize with our habits and tastes. Style, we are told, is the reflection of an age. It hardly needs to be proven that the discoveries of modern civilization have profoundly modified our manners, and that they resemble nothing that has been known in the past. . . . In our homes, from living room furniture to the oven in the kitchen, in the streets, from the lamp-post to the manhole cover, everything has been conceived by a designer. There are few things made by man that have not received the stamp of the artist. The disdain for modern decoration, then, is strange, to say the least. It is amazing that when all periods of the past have left their distinctive mark by particular styles, our century, which is so proud of its progress, humbly and slavishly contents itself with copying the decorative arts of the past. Deplorably enough, it is in fact only in our own country that such an apathy reigns. Other countries are working with fervour to create new styles, and they have produced truly complete and unified ensembles. . . . Today, we must find genuine support, and not just a show of generosity or benevolence. Having understood that the modern movement is not simply an aesthetic caprice, but answers a pressing need, a genuine necessity, and that it is a truly national cause, the public authorities, art-lovers, manufacturers, and the public must unite with artists and participate in the renovation of the French decorative arts and the creation of the styles of the twentieth century.[45]

1912

33. Henri Rapin, Poster.
Paris, musée de la Publicité.

1 March-1 April, Pavillon de Marsan

Catalogue cover: Henry de Waroquier

President: René Guilleré
Vice-presidents: Théodore Lambert,
Clément Mère
General Secretary: Geo Lamothe
Secretaries: Maurice Dufrène,
Henry de Waroquier
Treasurer: Georges Bourgeot

At the 1912 Salon, the Société's intensified effort to cultivate a modern style of decorative arts led to a change in admission restrictions, and a modification of its policy towards industry. Henceforth, "only those works will be accepted which are works of applied art, and which are clearly decorative in their composition, interpretation or destination. The works must demonstrate new tendencies; copies and imitations of past styles will be rigorously excluded."[46] To encourage a greater interest by potential manufacturers in designs by Société mem-

bers, the Salon catalogue now contained a special section devoted to the manufacturers ("éditeurs") rather than listing them only after the artist's name.[47]
A change in the overall aspect of the Salon can also be attributed to the fact that the designers were preparing for the Paris Exposition internationale des arts décoratifs scheduled for 1915. Calls by critics and reformers for a new style that was nevertheless based on French traditions of fine craftsmanship resulted in several extraordinary ensembles that were descendants of these traditions, particularly in their use of luxurious materials. The Salon's centrepiece was the small, oval *Salon* designed by René Lalique. Its walls were sheathed in porcelain tiles with platinum inlays and Louis XVI-inspired medaillons executed by the Manufacture de Sèvres. Paul Follot contributed an *Oval Boudoir*, decorated with maple inlaid work, a chimney in sculpted marble, and a niche in mosaic and wrought iron. The furniture

34. André Groult, Salon.

was sculpted and gilded. The furnishings in André Groult's *Salon* made references to the more bourgeois Louis-Philippe and French provincial styles, but the ensemble was enlivened by modern, floral printed fabrics whose bold colour combinations were inspired by Fauvist painting and the Ballets Russes.

Critic Louis Vauxcelles viewed the Salon as a victory of the modern style in France, and assured his readers, with more than a hint of chauvinism, that French designers had nothing to fear from their German competitors:

> The exhibition of the 'Artistes-Décorateurs' at the Pavillon de Marsan is a triumph. People come in droves; purchases and orders are on the rise. It would seem that the modernist ideas . . . are making headway, and that the victory of common sense is not far off. The exhibition of the Munich group at the 'Salon d'Automne' two years ago served as a powerful and effective stimulus to our French furniture-makers and ornamentalists. It is true, as we did not hesitate to point out then, the Bavarians lacked personality, grace and style. They systematically plagiarized the Empire, Louis-Philippe, English Louis XVI, Chippendale and Sheraton styles. In their ensembles we could see motifs from Belgium, Holland, Romania, and Czechoslovakia. The ensembles were heavy and featured discordant tonalities that shocked the eye. But what powerful discipline, and what homogeneity in their work, what a perfect subordination of the artisan to the 'artistic director', and also, what concern for technical achievement, what finish in the execution! This lesson was not lost. At the Salon d'Automne and in the Pavillon de Marsan, we felt the need to unite, to work together, to fight against the foreign competitor, not to lose hold of a movement that was born here and that should remain ours.[48]

36. Léon Jallot, Salon.

Above:

35. René Lalique, Oval Salon. Revetment in ceramic tiles with platinum inlays executed by the Manufacture nationale de Sèvres under the technical direction of René Lalique.

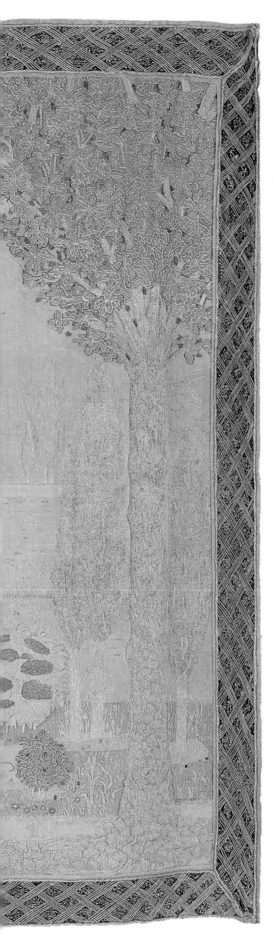

*37. Blanche Ory-Robin, Wall hanging,
1912. Embroidery on linen canvas.
Paris, musée d'Orsay.*

*38. Jubin O'Kin, Tea Caddy, 1910.
Sculpted and dyed wood, horn, gold.
Paris, musée d'Orsay.*

40. Eileen Gray, Les Magiciens de la nuit, lacquered wood panel with mother-of-pearl inlays.

39. Frantz Waldraff, Poster, 1913. Paris, musée de la Publicité.

22 February-31 March, Pavillon de Marsan

Organization of Salon:
Georges Bourgeot, Henri Simmen

President: Henry Marcel
Vice-presidents: Clément Mère,
Pierre Selmersheim,
Edouard Monod-Herzen
General Secretary: Geo Lamothe
Secretaries: Maurice Dufrène,
Emile Decoeur, Charles du Bosquet
Treasurer: Georges Bourgeot

Discussions on the possibility of an international exhibition of decorative arts to be held in Paris in 1915 sparked a series of violent debates between committee members of the Société and the Union centrale des art décoratifs, who had both developed the project, and members of the Paris City Council and representatives of the Parisian furniture industries. The debates centred principally on the definition of modernity. While the Société and Union centrale insisted upon including only "modern" works in the exhibition, thus preventing manufacturers from continuing to produce and exhibit copies of historical styles, the manufacturers themselves, seeing their interests threatened, argued that the government had no right to decide what was modern, or to exclude a large sector of the furnishing industries from this important international event.[49] The position of Faubourg manufacturers was defended by Alphonse Delville, president of the City Council, in a 1912 report. François Carnot, a deputy, president of the Union centrale, and one of the exhibition project's authors, published his response in the Société's 1913 Salon catalogue.[50] He blamed the resistance to a modern style on a small coalition of manufacturers who, lacking foresight, had only their immediate profit in mind. To assuage the fears of manufacturers, he tried to demonstrate that "modernity" did not necessarily mean a *tabula rasa*, but could be a natural evolution of tradition:

So, you think that our intentions are audacious, you have accused us of trying, through sheer will, to make a new and as yet unknown style spring from

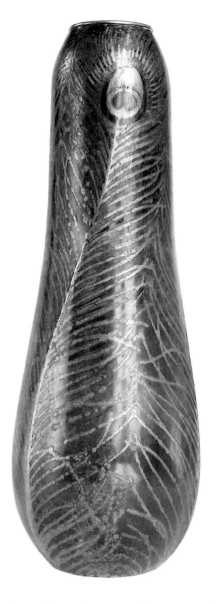

41. Jean Dunand, Vase. Copper repoussé with silver incrustations. Paris, musée des Arts décoratifs.

42. Alfred Bugniot, Cover for the Catalogue of the Eighth Salon des artistes décorateurs.

the earth. For that, you call us crazy and reckless. All of this simply because of the word 'modern'. Well, we must explain ourselves once and for all on this word which is brandished everywhere like a bogyman. Is modern art then an art that was born spontaneously, ignoring all tradition, oblivious to all techniques and to all past accomplishments of our race in the field of decoration? Which one of us can you accuse of ever having uttered such an absurdity? Each of our past styles, each new development in our artistic heritage down through the centuries was in its own day a modern style, a new formula that answered fresh economic, social or moral needs. This, in fact, is the only true definition of the term 'modern', which you are objecting to so vociferously. In every period, the modern style was the one that responded logically to the needs of the individual and collective life of the time. Our artistic tradition is but a long chain of which each link was modern in its day. This is the tradition that we must not allow to be interrupted.[51]

9eme SALON DE LA SOCIÉTÉ DES ARTISTES DÉCORATEURS DU 28 FÉVRIER AU 25 MARS MUSÉE DES ARTS DÉCORATIFS PAVILLON DE MARSAN LOUVRE

1914

28 February-25 March, Pavillon Marsan

Catalogue cover:
François-Louis Schmied
Organization of Salon:
Paul Follot, Clement Mère

President: Paul Vitry
Vice-presidents: Clément Mère,
Eugène Gaillard, Henri Rapin
General Secretary: Geo Lamothe
Secretaries: Edgar Brandt, Charles Hairon
Treasurer: Georges Bourgeot

In 1914, through the creation of a Committee of Patronage that included the President of the Republic, the Minister of Public Instruction and Fine Arts, the Minister of Commerce and Industry, deputies, senators, and private individuals like David David-Weill and the couturier and art collector Jacques Doucet, the Société was able to win additional government support.[52] This new initiative had the immediate effect of calling the work of the Société's members to the attention of government authorities for eventual commissions for interiors of public buildings. Société member Tony Selmersheim was chosen to design the offices of the president of the Paris City Council at the Hôtel de Ville—the first "modernist" chosen for a public commission.[53] At the annual salon the government made seven purchases—its largest number to date.
In spite of this, the 1914 Salon was one of the least successful in the view of the press, who found most of the interiors too theatrical. The *Salon* presented by Louis Süe and Jacques Palyart was highly criticized for its strange furnishings and its unsuccessful mixture of the bold colours and exoticism of the Ballets Russes with references to the Louis-Philippe style. These kinds of interiors led Fernand Roches,

43. Georges Barbier, Poster, 1914.
Paris, musée de la Publicité.

44. Eugénie O'Kin, Lotus blossom vase.
Engraved and sculpted ivory inlaid
with gold tacks.·Paris, musée d'Orsay.

45. Georges Bastard, Box.
Sculpted mother-of-pearl and ivory.
Paris, musée d'Orsay.

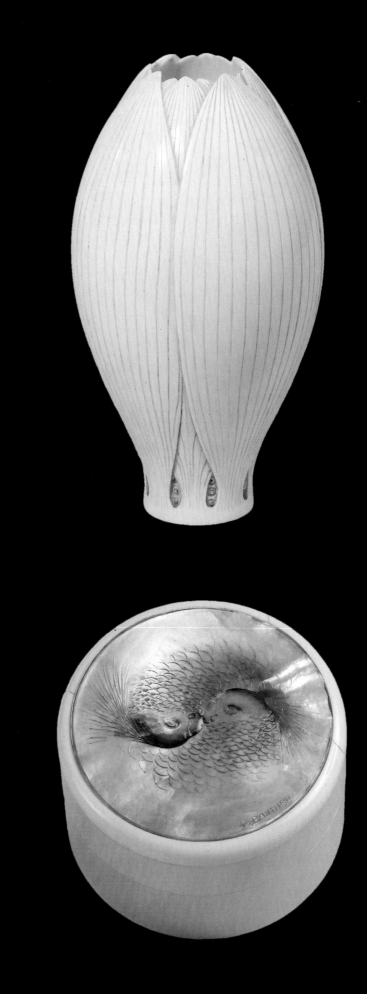

editor of the magazine *L'Art Décoratif*, to lament the decline of the longstanding French tradition of innovation and quality that he believed had disappeared in the 1830s—a decline that he attributed to a decadent society unaware of the realities of the twentieth century. In a passage that anticipated the aesthetics of the 1920s he imagined a future in which people would have furnishings that corresponded to their needs, produced by industry and enlightened by art:

This situation, which will put our times in a position of great *moral* inferiority in the eyes of history, has lasted for so many years that it hardly seems possible that it can continue any longer. Sometimes we have the feeling of witnessing the dawn of a new society. With it, new forms will appear that are awaiting their *raison d'être* and will constitute a fertile ground for the development of the applied arts. . . . A generation of idealistic and practical men is emerging that will help the decorative arts to escape from their chaotic situation by creating a new, utilitarian beauty for modern life. Tomorrow, the athletic youth of today will probably want furniture designed from a practical point of view, and not as an ephemeral theatre decor. . . . The decorative arts are psychological arts. The rhythm of the age, symbolized in wood, iron and clay, will spring from the new ways of living that we are now developing. Ornamentation as such will be abolished and become a simple function. Perhaps there will be no ornamentation at all—why not? Proportions alone will be the only signs of style, and man will express himself very naturally through an ordinary, everyday art, produced by an industry enlightened by aesthetic sentiment.[54]

47. Paul Follot, Bedroom. *Palisander.*

48. André Groult, Dining-room.
Burr elmwood.

49. Louis Süe and Jacques Palyart,
Salon. Amboyna, palisander,
marquetry in ebony and sycamore.

1919-1924

In 1911, the Société began planning an international exhibition of modern decorative arts to be held in Paris. This project originated in 1906 and was given a more precise form three years later by the art critic Roger Marx. It was the presentation of the Munich *Werkstätten* at the Salon d'Automne of 1910, however, that was the major impulse behind this initiative. The *Munichois* displayed simple, coordinated ensembles that, though somewhat heavy in style, were brightly coloured—perhaps too bright for some visitors. In any case, the show caused a sensation, and a counter-production by French artists was necessary, not only for aesthetic reasons but economically and nationally as well.

Artistic revolutions rocked the Parisian art world on the eve of the war. Enthusiastic praise was showered on the decors of the Ballets Russes of Serge Diaghilev, seen for the first time in Paris in 1909. Leon Bakst's decor for *Schéhérazade* in 1910 was at once sumptuous and barbaric, "simplified, reduced to a few lines and a play on two dominant and complementary colours, red and green, which blazed with light".[1] Pure colour, the basis of Fauvist painting, appeared on the stage before becoming a part of everyday life. On 20 February 1909, *Le Figaro* printed the Futurist Manifesto by the Italian poet Marinetti. Born in Italy, "for too long the great marketplace of second-hand goods", the Futurist movement attacked conventions in literature, music, and the visual arts. It threw movement and speed into pictorial space, and acclaimed the machine age.

Rich with these new elements, the artistes décorateurs used a new range of forms and decors and a palette of dense, saturated colours. From the Werkstätten displays, they had learned to create ensembles instead of collections of disparate objects, and the importance of working together on group projects. At the same time Société members were hired to direct the applied arts workshops for the big Paris department stores. Two of these, the Galeries Lafayette and Le Bon Marché, hired Maurice Dufrène and Paul Follot as directors. Both designers had been members of the Société since its foundation, and had worked before 1900 at the Maison Moderne founded by the art critic Julius Meier-Graefe. The model for these studios was the galerie de l'Art Nouveau, founded in 1895 by the Oriental-art dealer, Siegfried Bing, after a trip to the United States where he had especially admired the work of Tiffany. He believed that the public should not be presented with individual objects like isolated pieces of furniture, but with complete interiors designed by different artists, all coordinated by one artistic director. Bing's Art Nouveau Pavilion at the 1900 Exposition Universelle illustrated the penchant of the French participants for high-quality craftsmanship rather than for mass production.

The department store Le Printemps assigned the direction of its own applied arts workshops, Primavera, to a former president of the

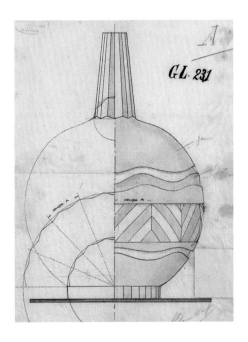

51. Maurice Dufrène, Study for a glass bottle designed for La Maîtrise, executed by the cristalleries Saint-Louis, 1923. Saint-Louis-lès-Bitche, Archives of the cristalleries Saint-Louis.

50. Jean Dupas, Study for the poster and catalogue cover for the 15th Salon of the Société des artistes décorateurs, 1924. Charcoal and watercolour.

Société, René Guilleré. The Galeries Lafayette opened La Maîtrise in 1921 with Maurice Dufrène, followed by the Bon Marché's Pomone, directed by Paul Follot, while Studium of the Grands Magasins du Louvre was entrusted to two young designers, Etienne Kohlmann and Maurice Matet. These studios were so successful that they had their own pavilions at the 1925 Exhibition.

Faced with the great upheavals of the First World War, the Société tried to restore to France its leading role by holding an international fair in Paris. Here the Société took a resolutely modern position and made an effort to absorb the new ideologies. The postwar years were prosperous for the Société, which benefited from Paris's position as a cultural Mecca for Dada, the Ballets Russes rejuvenated by Jean Cocteau, Picasso, the Groupe de Six, and the Surrealist movement. The Société Salons, however, did not always show this effervescence, reflecting, rather, the adherence to French classicism by its members. The 1924 Salon, intended as a rehearsal for the international competition of 1925, was an exception to the Société's usual preference for luxury and one-of-a-kind pieces, at least in the section entitled *Reception and private rooms of a modern apartment*, organized with Pierre Chareau with the participation of Robert Mallet-Stevens (the architect chosen by the de Noailles for the construction of their summer villa in Hyères), and Pierre Legrain, who created a completely

52. Scene from the Ballet Chout, *performed in Paris in 1921 by the Ballets Russes. Produced by Serge Diaghilev, sets and costumes by Michel Larionov.*

53. Catalogue for La Maîtrise, applied arts workshops of the Galeries Lafayette, directed by Maurice Dufrène, 1922. Paris, Library of the musée des Arts décoratifs.

original interior to house the fashion designer Jacques Doucet's collections of Tribal and Oriental art and Cubist and Surrealist paintings. The group of men and women who participated in this exhibit—architects, decorators, painters, sculptors—belonged to the modern world that had grown from the aesthetic revolutions of the beginning of the twentieth century.

The 1924 Salon highlighted the differences that would lead to the Société's split in 1929. According to critic Guillaume Janneau, before the 1925 Exhibition the artistes décorateurs were divided into two camps: the "contemporaries" and the "moderns". The contemporaries claimed to be part of the French tradition that stretched back to the reign of Louis-Philippe and even further in the eighteenth century. They championed the cause of quality, hoping to erase the memory of the disastrous productions of the second half of the nineteenth century. The moderns were less concerned with style than with architectural space and the design of the furniture that would occupy it. Nevertheless, on the eve of the 1925 Exhibition, the moderns were still intrigued by fine materials and an abstract and geometric type of decor. While they distinguished themselves from the contemporaries by opting for ensembles, they had not yet gone over to pure functionalism—and some of them never would.

Yvonne Brunhammer

54. *Henri Rapin, Back cover of the catalogue of the 1919 Salon of the Société des artistes décorateurs with advertising for the Grands Magasins du Louvre.*

The end of the First World War left France with conflicting attitudes towards modernity and tradition. The main thrust of post-war artistic activity was aimed at recapturing or reformulating the past, through a notion of a *retour à l'ordre* which manifested itself in almost all areas of cultural activity.[1] This return to order celebrated qualities considered traditionally French—classicism and rationalism—which were thought to constitute the very essence of the national identity. Many began to define and analyse the specifically French qualities that should be safeguarded in the post-war era, because it was widely believed that it was French Civilization that had won the war against the forces of barbarity.

One of the first demands for a return to order in the decorative arts was made by André Vera in an article entitled "The Decorative Doctrine of Tomorrow", published in *Le Matin* in November 1918. Vera believed that the war had swept away the confusion existing in both artistic and national life before 1914, and that a new and unified modern style could now be established:

> Our next decorative style will not perpetuate these manners from former times, but in the future, it will have to guard itself against vanity. The designer will therefore be wary of French *légèreté*: we will have to rejoice with gravity. . . . This is why designers will have to present themselves as having made peace with one another, who have affection for one another, who will be subject to one another: in other words, they should work as though they were part of a confraternity. They will express this accord by the development, not of individual themes, but of a common theme, an ensemble of forms and colours whose goal will be to awaken and channel the energies of the nation in a particular and French way.[2]

To achieve this, he explained, artists must be disciplined. They must not only work with one another, but must submit to the overriding authority of the architect. Geometry, he continued, would be the language shared by the artist and the architect, and a stylistic unity would be achieved only by adhering to traditional rules of composition—rules which, through their logic and correctness, satisfied universal needs rather than individual sentiments. Urging designers to fulfill their roles as "artisans of the indispensible intellectual and moral reform" of the post-war era, he underlined the importance of the patient work of the craftsman in this reform.

> The next style will be charged not with nonchalance, but with an obstinate and manly vigour: lightness, precipitation and inconstancy will no longer be in season; patient work will have to be done before the desire for it will pass.[3]

Like Vera, few artists and designers who envisioned a modern, post-war style of domestic furnishings saw the end of the war as the beginning of a utopian era free of the legacy of the past. In spite of the fact that more than 300,000 buildings had been damaged or destroyed during the war, few Parisian decorators saw this situation as a possibility to create something really new. In fact, at a time when hundreds of thousands of homes needed to be built and furnished, little was said in the Parisian milieu of decorative arts about reconstruction. The 1919 and 1920 volumes of the leading decorative arts review *Art et Décoration* carried only one article on prefabricated housing, and nothing about the furnishings needed to complete them.[4] The rest of the articles hardly differed from those of pre-war issues. It was almost as if nothing had happened.

The outbreak of the war brought a halt to the Salons of the Société des artistes décorateurs until 1919. The committee, however, provided services for members remaining on the home front by holding a weekly reunion at the musée des Arts décoratifs, and through the creation of an emergency fund.[5] The Société's honorary president, the *médailleur* Emile-Séraphin Vernier, assumed the direction during the four years of hostilities. At the end of the war only the Société made an organized attempt to respond to the demands of reconstruction. As soon as the Armistice was declared, it began planning its next Salon, publishing a call for works in December 1919. Designer Tony Selmersheim took on the task of directing the tenth Salon that opened at the musée des Arts décoratifs on 28 March 1919. The proposed theme was "to help repair the damage of the war by developing simple models for furniture for the reconstruction of the devastated regions".[6] Inaugurating a new era of peace and stability, the Salon provided a much-needed distraction for war-weary Parisians: more than 18,000 visitors attended in six weeks, as opposed to 7,250 at the salon of 1914.[7]

One of the Société's main tasks after the war was to attract a new generation of decorative artists, and to persuade industry and commerce to participate in its efforts to diffuse a modern style of decorative arts. Thus, in 1919 the Société accepted advertising in its catalogue for the first time: the back cover was purchased by the Grands Magasins du Louvre, whose advertisement was integrated into a decorative floral design by Henri Rapin. The Société also showed a new attitude towards cooperation with manufacturers by opening a special sales office, and by allowing the exhibitors to form a more direct relationship with the consumer by listing their addresses, as well as those of their collaborators and manufacturers, on the labels for their stands. They were also permitted to indicate whether or not their works were produced in series, and even the prices. The committee stressed the importance of this new policy:

The times are over when the Société was only concerned with making art for art's sake, lecturing the public and guiding its taste towards new trends. Today, when all of the knowledgeable people are going modern, it is no longer a matter of platonic manifestations, but of realizations. There is no longer any doubt that, while maintaining a seemly artistic character in our exhibition, we will have to organize ourselves practically for the sale of our works.[8]

55. Eugénie O'Kin, Poppy flower vase, 1919 Salon. Sculpted, engraved, and painted ivory; jade and silver. Paris, musée d'Orsay.

56. *Louis Süe et André Mare,* Dining-room,
*1919. Furniture mass-produced and sold through
catalogue by the Compagnie des arts français.*

57. *André Fréchet,* Dining-room, *1919.*

58. *Gaston Le Bourgeois,* Child's Bedroom,
1919. Painted and sculpted wood.

The 1919 Salon held the highly symbolic value of being the first major gathering of decorative artists since 1914. By showing the works of the artists who had been popular before the war, it was above all a reassuring sign that things were returning to normal, and as the Société's new president, Paul Vitry (1872-1941), curator of sculpture at the Louvre, and professor at the Ecole nationale des arts décoratifs pointed out, France was ready to enter the post-war "artistic and economic struggle".[9] Due to a lack of time and organization, however, only a few decorators responded to the call for a *mobilier à bon marché* (inexpensive furnishings), working in tandem with those factories which had supplied the war machine and that were now trying to convert to peacetime production. Théodore Lambert contributed furniture for a dining-room and bedroom destined for farmhouses that could be bought in kits and assembled with screws. Ensembles by Louis Süe and André Mare in lacquered grey poplar, decorated with a simple, geometric floral motif placed centrally on oval panels were among the most successful at the Salon. The furnishings were assured of a large distribution —they could be ordered by catalogue from Süe and Mare's newly-founded Compagnie des arts français.[19]

In July 1919, as part of the national project for post-war recovery, the government resumed plans for the international exhibition of modern decorative arts first initiated by the Société in 1911. The government hoped to ensure the development of the luxury industries on which an important sector of the national economy depended, and to prevent the proletarization of those skilled artisans whose livelihoods had been interrupted by the war. The statement published on the exhibition project by Léon Riotor, Paris City Councillor, demonstrates how important the *industries de luxe* and the maintenance of highly skilled labour were to the national economy, and how the exhibition could preserve and develop them:

> Concern for our industry and our national prosperity makes an urgent appeal necessary for the defence of French taste. Arts applied to industry (wrongly termed decorative arts) will be henceforth at the heart of our effort. Since we are no longer major producers, let us at least be tasteful ones. In this way we will be able to resist foreign overproduction and give to certain highly esteemed, but rare, craftsmen the support they deserve.[11]

The Société saw the resumption of the exhibition project, now scheduled for 1923 (later postponed until 1925), as a sign of official approval of its goal of promoting a modern style and winning public acceptance. But the association still needed the cooperation of industrialists, who were often reluctant to hire the best designers and take the time and financial investment required to produce new models:

> Our artist-creators have long asserted their will to modernity. . . . If modern art has an existence and already a history, it is thanks to them and to their relentless efforts. Yet they cannot do everything alone. Modern art must not only be something for exhibitions and museums; it must live a real life profitable for all; it needs the indispensible aid of industry which, respecting the unquestioned rights and personality of all inventors, will come to choose these designs, perfect them, and diffuse them throughout the world.[12]

Even though the Société's ideal was to work closely with industry to diffuse modern design to the general public, the Salons of the immediate post-war years continued to be dominated by one-of-a-kind pieces requiring luxurious materials and fine craftsmanship. By 1920, what is now considered the

Art Deco style was in full bloom, and the *esprit de géometrie* that André Vera evoked in 1918 could be seen in virtually every domain of decorative arts.[13] The dressing table exhibited by Paul Follot at the 1920 Salon is a striking example of the treatment of ornament and materials that characterized this new trend. As opposed to the naturalistic climbing stems and flowers typical of Art Nouveau, Follot's design seemed inspired by Vera's ideas: the carved floral ornaments were geometricized, gathered into inverted cornucopias to form the mirror frame, and juxtaposed against the triangular forms of the trellis-like structure of the frame's support. The gracious, curving forms and gilding made vague references to French historical styles. The geometricized flower, influenced by the pre-war designs of the Wiener Werkstätte and the couturier Paul Poiret, became one of the most popular decorative motifs of the new style, and could be found everywhere: on porcelain services designed by Jean Luce, the elegant engraved or enameled glassware by Maurice Marinot (1920 and 1921 Salons), on forged ironwork by Raymond Subes (1920 and 1922 Salons) and in carpet and fabric designs by Maurice Dufrène (1922 Salon) and Paul Vera (the brother of André). In 1922 Pierre Chareau introduced decorative cubism into furnishings. Their multifaceted, smooth surfaces implied a machine aesthetic, even though Chareau's work was often finely crafted by hand in rich materials. Between 1912 and 1922, the major Parisian department stores joined the battle to make modern furnishings available at low prices to a large public by opening their own applied arts workshops. Headed by some of the most eminent Parisian artists, the ateliers designed, manufactured, and sold original and frequently innovative designs. This trend was initiated by the Société's founder, René Guilleré, when he resigned in 1912 to found the Atelier Primavera for Printemps department store. His wife, Charlotte Chauchet-Guilleré, headed the group of designers until the late 1920s. The Galeries Lafayette opened an atelier in 1921—La Maîtrise, directed by Maurice Dufrène, who had been a member of the Société since its foundation. Next came La Pomone (1923) of the Bon Marché store, directed by Société member Paul Follot, and Studium (1924), for the Grands Magasins du Louvre, directed by two young graduates of the Ecole Boulle, Etienne Kohlmann and Maurice Matet.[14] In 1922, Chauchet-Guilleré and Dufrène made their first important contributions to the Société's Salon as representatives of the department stores, showing simple, moderately-priced ensembles. For the Salon of 1923, eleven designers represented stores, and the presence of these *ateliers d'art appliqué* became increasingly important with each successive Salon. In 1922, the Société resumed its campaign to elevate the decorative artist's professional status by petitioning the government for official recognition as a public utility. It also tried to obtain an independent Salon in the Grand Palais equal to the prestigious fine arts Salons such as those of the Société des artistes français and the Société nationale des beaux-arts.[15] They hoped to further their cause by nominating a new president who occupied an important position within the government, and who could act as an intermediary between the Société and the public authorities. In 1923, Maurice Bokanowski (1879-1928), reporter-general of the government Finance Commission, accepted the Société's invitation to become its president.[16] Largely through his intervention, the association realized its first autonomous Salon in the Grand Palais in 1923, and was recognized as a public utility in 1924.

59. Paul Follot, Detail of Dressing Table, illustrated fig. 81, 1920.

60. *Maurice Marinot,* Flasks and Vase, *1921. Engraved glass.*

One bastion remained to be conquered. The central goal of the Société, one that had been at the heart of the applied arts movement since the mid-nineteenth century, was to bridge the gap between the "major" and "minor" arts. It still had not been able to win a fine arts status for its members because of one important administrative detail. Although the Society benefitted from some financial support from the Administration of Fine Arts, the decorative arts depended upon the jurisdiction of the Ministry of Commerce. It was because of the inevitably commercial aspect of the decorative arts and the relationship that individual members were forced to maintain with more powerful interest groups like the Chambre syndicale d'ameublement, the union of manufacturers of the Faubourg Saint-Antoine, that the decorators found their longing for fine artist status frustrated.

61. *Raymond Subes,* Radiator cover, *1922.*

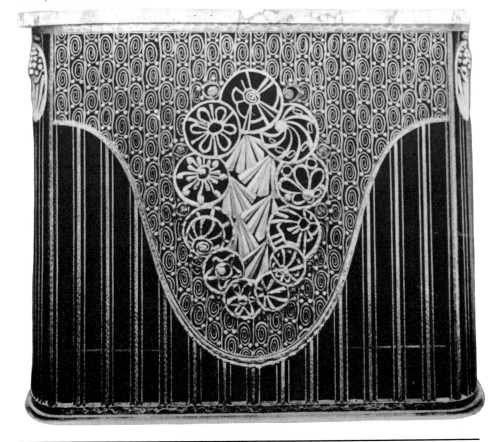

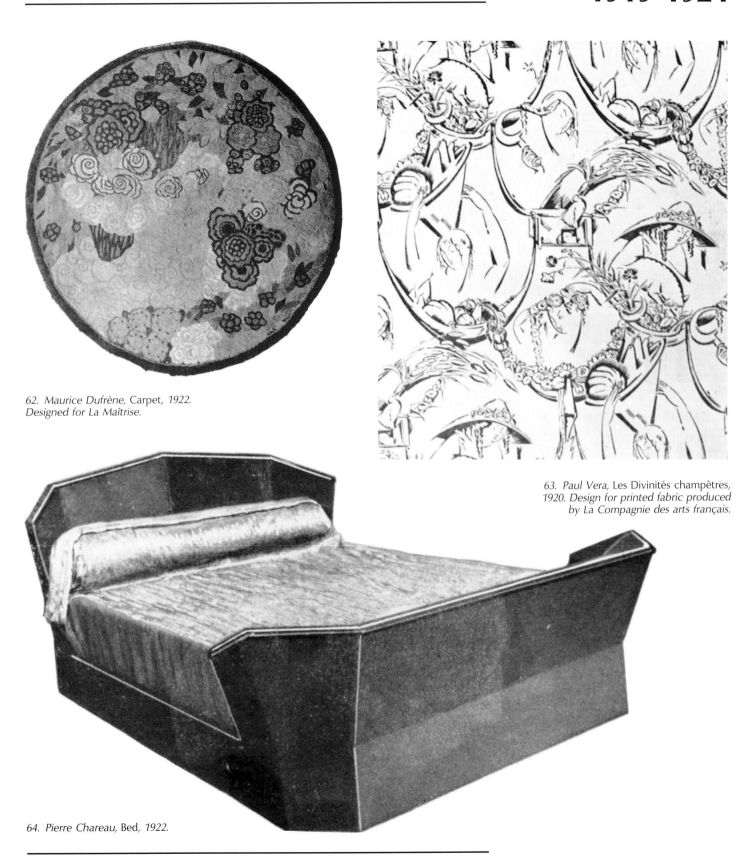

62. Maurice Dufrène, Carpet, 1922.
Designed for La Maîtrise.

63. Paul Vera, Les Divinités champêtres,
1920. Design for printed fabric produced
by La Compagnie des arts français.

64. Pierre Chareau, Bed, 1922.

The effects of this difficult and ambiguous situation became evident in 1924 when the Société was preparing its contribution to the 1925 Exposition des arts décoratifs. Already anxious to distinguish the works created by Société artists from those of the more common industrialists, they distrusted the increasing role that merchants and industrialists were playing in the organization of the exhibition. In addition, the Société felt that the principle that was to underlay the exhibition, "to create an alliance between artists and industrialists", was not defined clearly enough and would lead to a serious misunderstanding on the part of a public not yet sophisticated enough to distinguish between true examples of modern decorative arts, and the cheaper, often poor-quality copies produced by Faubourg manufacturers.

The Société became increasingly concerned when numerous Faubourg industrialists were elected to the juries of the 1925 Exposition, and feared the commercial concerns of manufacturers would dominate the event. The Société was convinced that the imitation of modern design was as detrimental to the French decorative arts movement as the pastiches of ancient styles. As is clear from the comments addressed to the General Assembly of 1924 by vice-president Charles Hairon, after a brief post-war rapprochement the Société began to assume an increasingly distant position in relation to industry. He encouraged the members to insist on quality, and to maintain the fine art image that the Société had always tried to project:

It will have been understood that there was a spiritual force in our

65. Jean Puiforcat, Bonbonnière, *1923. Paris, galerie Suger.*

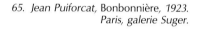

66. Jean Puiforcat, Lamp, *1922 Salon. Silver, glass and ivory. Paris, J. Brugnot Collection.*

67. *Maurice Dufrène,* Modern Interior, *1922. Designed for La Maîtrise.*

group whose strength rose in parallel with that of industry. This strength is the strength of men who, by a slow but continuous effort, create new forms that generate life and prosperity. It will also have been understood that the age-old formula of the 'artist subservient to the industrial patron who pays him', had to be replaced by the more just and appropriate formula used by the artists and industrialists who work with us: 'industrial might put at the service of creative thought'. . . . We thought that in a solemn display of the activity of France, it was not enough to see only those works destined for

the familiar context of everyday life. There also had to be works for the 'Elite', the elite which made for the fame and glory of France, those for whom art is a spiritual value and whose works are the sincere expression of a true emotion. . . .[17]

The Société counted on the Salon of 1924 to be an important public demonstration of its artistic solidarity and its high ideals, and a means of showing the Commission of the 1925 Exposition of Decorative Arts that the Société should play a leading role in this important international competition. The press considered it the most successful in the Société's history. The architec-

68. Charlotte Chauchet-Guilleré,
Bedroom, 1922. Palisander.
Designed for Primavera.

69. Claudius Linossier, Vases, 1924.
Hammered metal, copper
and silver incrustations.

70. Georges Barbier, Le Rendez-vous, 1920.
Silk brocade. Designed for Bianchini-Férier.

71. Jean Dunand, Vase shown in the Rotunda
by Henri Rapin, 1924.

tural setting designed by Louis-Pierre Sézille was more imposing than that of previous Salons and provided a dramatic backdrop for the individual works. Brasswares (*dinanderie*) and ceramic work were given places of honour. The large vase by Jean Dunand that occupied the rotunda of the entrance hall was hammered from one sheet of metal, and was one of the artist's most monumental works to date. On a smaller scale, the vases and plates in metal with incrustations of copper and silver by Claudius Linossier charmed visitors by the purity of their profiles and the delicacy of their geometric decoration. Although the general tendency in furniture was towards straight lines, smooth undecorated surfaces and monumental proportions, typified by the bedroom ensemble presented by Louis Sognot for the Atelier Primavera, or the Cubist-inspired grand piano by René Prou, manufactured by Pleyel, there were still a number of artists using sculpted wood ornament. André Frechet, director of the Ecole Boulle, explained that decorative wood sculpture was an eminently French art, and that it was necessary to find modern applications for the great tradition of *ébénisterie* in spite of calls for simpler forms and unadorned surfaces adapted to serial production.[18]

The centrepiece of the Salon, however, and the Société's most unified statement yet, was the group presentation assembled by Pierre Chareau entitled, *Réception et l'intimité d'un appartement moderne*. It was conceived to respond to the requirements of the upcoming 1925 exhibition—to show the decorative arts in complete, related settings created by a group of designers under the guidance of one artistic director. Robert Mallet-Stevens designed the vestibule, a large space of sparse geometry, enlivened only by four cubic light fixtures suspended

from the ceiling. Pierre Legrain, known for his luxurious bookbindings, contributed an office/library decorated with the African-influenced furnishings he had just designed for the couturier Jacques Doucet. A luxurious hall and dining-room were presented by Jacques-Emile Ruhlmann, and Paul Poiret showed a veranda decorated with large cushions that drew on the pre-war exotic, Orientalist style of his Maison Martine. Francis Jourdain displayed a small armchair and desk in the unpretentious and bare, geometric style for which he had been known since 1913. The most spectacular interior was the bedroom designed by

Chareau, decorated with geometricized furnishings, and Cubist-inspired carpets and fabrics by Eileen Gray. The success of this ensemble by Chareau, Mallet-Stevens, Jourdain, Gray, and Legrain would lead to their split from the Société in 1929 to found the Union des artistes modernes.[19]

The success of the Salon encouraged the Administration of Fine Arts to grant the Société a subsidy for its participation at the 1925 Exposition des arts décoratifs. The centrepiece of the Exposition, it would be the crowning achievement of the Société's struggle to establish a modern French style.

Suzanne Tise

72. Henri Rapin, Rotonde, 1924.

73. Louis-Pierre Sezille, Hall, 1924.

75. Pierre Legrain, Study with furniture designed for Jacques Doucet, *1924.*

74. Pierre Legrain, Chair designed for Jacques Doucet, *1924. Oak. Paris, musée des Arts décoratifs.*

1919

28 March-30 April, Pavillon Marsan

Catalogue cover: Henri Rapin

Organization of Salon:
Tony Selmersheim, Edgar Brandt

President: Paul Vitry
Vice-presidents: Clément Mère,
Eugène Gaillard, Henri Rapin
General Secretary: Geo Lamothe
Secretaries: Edgar Brandt, Charles Hairon
Treasurer: Georges Bourgeot

Paris was still under military authority when the Société's tenth Salon opened in March 1919, and restrictions remained in force for food and fuel.[20] But as Paul Vitry explained, organizing a Salon so soon after the Armistice, in spite of these difficult conditions, the Société would demonstrate that it could respond to the demands, both material and moral, of Reconstruction.

Without preventing our members from showing their usual work we proposed that they present projects or fully-realized designs intended to aid in a dignified reconstruction of the regions devastated by the War. . . . It should be pointed out that our Society is one of the very first to present itself before the judgement of the public, thereby resuming the flow of progress interrupted by the War and reaffirming our former ambitions. It would be superfluous to reiterate these ambitions one by one, but it is obvious that they are now just as important as ever, that the originality of creation, the quality of execution, and the diffusion of designs by manufacturers made possible by a loyal agreement with industrialists, are more

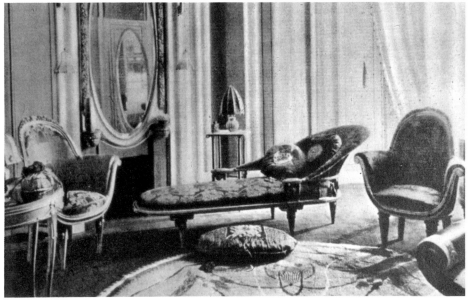

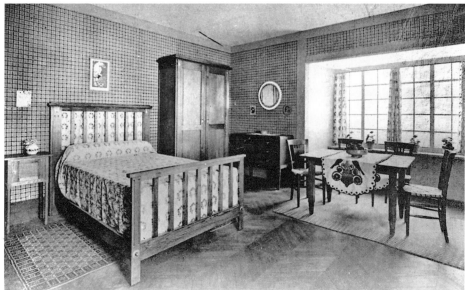

than ever the order of the day. A few months ago, France's main problem was survival. Today it must prosper, it must win the economic and artistic struggle as it won the military struggle, and we want to help with all the means in our power.[21]

If the theme of the Salon was the Reconstruction, it was in fact a salon of contrasts. Only a few designers responded to the call for furnishings for the devastated regions. Of the contributions that were made, however, one of the most important was Louis Süe's and André Mare's mass-produced bedroom and dining-room made of standardized wood elements. Sold by catalogue, they were manufactured by Borel and Savary, an aviation company that had been a wartime supplier and that was now attempting to keep its factories open through the furniture business. Wood

sculptor and artist Gaston Le Bourgeois worked with the toy manufacturer Jouets de France (which hired the war-wounded as artisans) on painted wood furnishings for children. Mathieu Gallerey pursued his research on simple and inexpensive furnishings. It was at this Salon that the decorative arts production workshops of the Parisian department stores made their debut. Galeries Lafayette commissioned Tony Selmersheim to design a series of inexpensive furnishings for a bedroom and dining-room in polished and painted wood. In contrast, a number of designers exhibited luxurious and beautifully-crafted works. Maurice Dufrène showed a sumptuous seven-piece ensemble in which the *Boudoir*, combining maple and gilded wood, and decorated with carved roses, fully illustrated what would become known as the Art Deco style.

77. Maurice Dufrène, Dining-room, 1919.

78. Maurice Dufrène, Boudoir, 1919. Maple, lacquered and gilt wood.

79. Mathieu Gallerey, Bedroom.

1920

26 February-31 March 1920,
Pavillon de Marsan

Catalogue cover:
Marguerite de Félice
Poster: Adrien Karbowsky
Organization of Salon:
Louis-Pierre Sezille, Georges Bastard

President: Paul Vitry
Vice-presidents: Théodore Lambert,
Henri Rapin, Emile Decoeur
General Secretary: Geo Lamothe
Secretaries: Georges Bastard,
Eugène Capon

81. Paul Follot, Coiffeuse and chair.
Sculpted and gilt wood, marble. Paris,
musée d'Art moderne de la Ville de Paris.

82. Maurice Dufrène, Sideboard. Mahogany,
black lacquer and marquetry.

80. Paul Follot, Salon/Studio.

1921

4 March-17 April, Pavillon de Marsan

President: Paul Vitry
Vice-presidents: Théodore Lambert,
Henri Rapin, Emile Decoeur
General Secretary: Geo Lamothe
Secretaries: Georges Bastard,
Eugène Capon

83. *Louis Doumergue et Albert Borgeaud,*
Dining-room.

84. *Francis Jourdain,* Dining-room.

85. Henri Rapin, Dining-room.

86. Maurice Dufrène, Drawing for
a commode and chair illustrated
in the catalogue of the 12th Salon.

LA S^{te} DES ARTISTES DECORATEURS

DU 30 AVRIL AU 30 JUIN

ANDRÉ GROULT

AU SALON DES ARTISTES FRANÇAIS

1922

30 April-30 June, Grand Palais, in conjunction with the Salon of the Société des artistes français

Organization of Salon:
Jacques-Emile Ruhlmann, Charles Hairon

President: Paul Vitry
Vice-presidents: Theodore Lambert,
René Kieffer, Emile Decoeur
General Secretary and Treasurer:
Geo Lamothe
Secretaries: Georges Bastard,
Eugène Capon

87. André Groult, Poster.
Paris, musée de la Publicité.

88. Léon Jallot, Dining-room.

89. Maurice Dufrène, Dining-room.
Walnut and zebra wood
Designed for La Maîtrise.

livened by modernized tapestry design by Charles Dufresne, produced by Aubusson. In his silver pieces, Jean Puiforcat took a new and rigorous approach to the object, favouring volumes, fluid lines, and smooth reflective surfaces rather than surface decoration. For his hammered copper *Tea Service* Jean Dunand sought lively decorative motifs inspired by the forms that he was decorating. He gave more life to his surfaces by using coloured patinas and incrustations of softer metals.

By 1922, the Arts and Crafts aspect that had dominated the Salon mostly disappeared and many designers were cooperating with manufacturers to produce their designs in series. The decorative arts workshops of the Parisian department stores presented important displays: Maurice Dufrène, who had just become director of La Maîtrise workshop of Galeries Lafayette, showed a dining room in polished oak including a buffet, table and six chairs that sold for what was at the time a modest sum of 1,250 francs. Charlotte Chauchet-Guilleré, the wife of the Société's founder, representing Primavera, the workshop of Printemps, contributed a dining-room in rosewood with ivory marquetry. The buffet, table and two chairs sold for 6,850 francs. The clean lines and smooth surfaces of the furnishings were distinctly modern—though the addition of motifs in ivory marquetry drawn from Greek pottery designs were directed towards a middle-class buying public used to copies of historical styles to convince them that the modern and the traditional could be combined. Louis Süe and André Mare's furnishings, however, were clearly traditional. The small *Canape* in gilded wood recalled eighteenth-century models, but was en-

91. View of the Salon installation, *Grand Palais*.

*92. Louis Süe et André Mare, Canapé.
Gilt wood, tapestry executed by Aubusson
after a cartoon by Charles Dufresne.*

93. Paul Follot, Salon.

1923

3 May-1 July, Grand Palais

President: Maurice Bokanowski
Vice-presidents: Charles Hairon,
Paul Follot, Henri Rapin
General Secretary and Treasurer:
Geo Lamothe
Secretaries:
Léon-Emile Bouchet, Laurent Malclès

*94. Pierre Legrain, Table designed
for Jacques Doucet. Palisander veneer,
top painted to simulate egg-shell lacquer.
Paris, musée des Arts décoratifs.*

96. *Pierre Chareau,*
Children's corner. *Wicker.*

P.CHAREAU

95. *Pierre Chareau,* Drawing for Table
and Chairs in Wicker for a Children's Corner.
Paris, musée des Arts décoratifs.

98. Francis Jourdain, Dining-room.
Oak and zebra wood.

99. Lucie Renaudot, Bedroom.
Painted and gilt wood.

97. Maurice Dufrène, Dining-room.
Designed for La Maîtrise.

1924

8 May-8 July, Grand Palais

Organization of Salon: Louis-Pierre Sézille,
Henri Rapin, Maurice Dufrène

President: Maurice Bokanowski
Vice-presidents: Charles Hairon,
Henri Rapin, Maurice Dufrène
General Secretary: Geo Lamothe
Secretaries: Fernand Nathan,
Raymond Subes
Treasurer: Léon Bouchet

The 1924 Salon was a trial run for the
Société for its international competition of
the following year. Frantz Jourdain, founder
of the Salon d'Automne and member of
Société's patronage committee, insisted in
his introduction to the Salon catalogue
that the success of the exhibition would
depend on a close alliance between artists
and industrialists, with the artist playing the
leading role:

> Will this exhibition succeed in
> demonstrating once and for all the
> necessity of a close cooperation be-
> tween artists and industrialists? The
> modern movement was created by
> artists, and by artists only. It would be
> only fair not to forget this. Apart from
> five or six exceptions, it has been viol-
> ently attacked by industrialists, who, out

100. Jacques-Emile Ruhlmann, Chiffonier.
Amboyna wood with ivory marquetry.
Paris, galerie Arc-en-Seine.

101. Paul Follot, Music room.
Designed for La Pomone.

102. Jean Dupas, Catalogue cover.

SOCIÉTÉ DES ARTISTES DÉCORATEURS

CATALOGUE
DU
XVᵉᵐᵉ SALON

GRAND PALAIS DES CHAMPS-ÉLYSÉES
DU 8 MAI AU 8 JUILLET 1924

of routine, egotism, a lack of foresight or intelligence, obstinately refused to extricate themselves from the historical styles that have been so lucrative. . . . But will this exhibition of 1925, which is completely ours, achieve the results we have hoped for? Will its success not be followed by cruel disappointments? After all, ideas have progressed and I strongly hope that industrialists, many of whom have the volition, will recognize that their salvation lies in a union with artists.[22]

Above all the Société wanted to demonstrate that it was a coherent, though heterogeneous, group of creators, and it tried to revise the monotonous aspect of the string of individual stands usually designed for the Salon. It chose Louis-Pierre Sézille, Pierre Chareau and Maurice Dufrène to develop a new arrangement that would satisfy the entire corps of decorators. The *Rotunda* by Henri Rapin led into the exhibition spaces and theatrically accentuated a masterpiece of *dinanderie* by Jean Dunand. The spaces between the double columns housed isolated pieces of fine cabinetwork such as the *Chiffonnier* by Jacques-Emile Ruhlmann.

The *Grand Hall* by Sézille was brightened by vividly painted columns and pilasters. Dufrène organized a gallery of showcases and stretched a drapery across the ceiling to create a dramatic, trapezoidal space. The exhibits aimed for an atmosphere of theatricality that would become typical of interior design during the late 1920s and 1930s. Paul Follot's monumental *Music*

103. Henri Rapin, Rotunda.

104. Robert Mallet-Stevens, Vestibule.

Room designed for La Pomone, the design workshop of the Bon Marché department store, displayed luxurious furnishings in palisander, ebony and gilt wood. For the Louvre department store, Maurice Matet designed a bathroom, a domestic space rarely treated by decorators, in which he elevated the bathtub onto a podium placed within a niche. The ceramic panels, adorned with a Cubist floral design, were created by Jan and Jöel Martel.

The ensemble that attracted the most attention at the Salon was organized by Pierre Chareau, who directed Robert Mallet-Stevens, Francis Jourdain, Eileen Gray, Pierre Legrain, Paul Poiret and Jacques-Emile Ruhlmann. Pierre Legrain contributed an *Office-library* furnished with the works that he had designed for the couturier Jacques Doucet. The African-inspired *Chair*, *Drum Table* and the ebony desk with a *galuchat* writing surface were the perfect design solutions for Doucet's collections of modern and tribal art. Pierre Chareau showed a *Salon* and adjoining *Bedroom*; the Salon was furnished with a divan and chairs with cubist-faceted profiles. The floating alabaster planes of the sculptural floor lamp *La Religeuse*, suggested a Cubist exploration of the fourth dimension. The salon was completed with paintings and sculptures by Georges Braque, Henri Laurens, Picasso, and Dunoyer de Segonzac, while the chimney was fitted out with sculptural andirons by Jacques Lipschitz. Mallet-Stevens created the vestibule, a space strongly influenced both by his Viennese experience and de Stijl architecture.

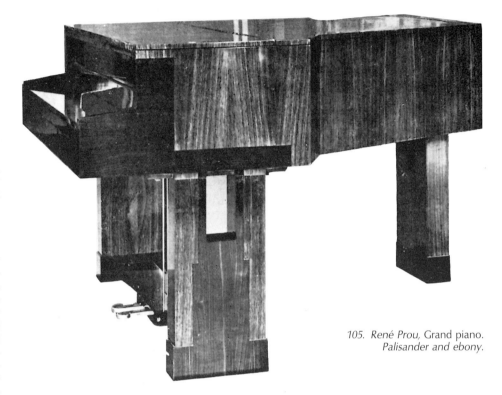

105. René Prou, Grand piano. Palisander and ebony.

106. Pierre Chareau, Bedroom. Andirons by Jacques Lipschitz, carpets by Eileen Gray.

MINISTÈRE DU COMMERCE ET DE L'INDUSTRIE

EXPOSITION
INTERNATIONALE
ARTS DÉCORATIFS
ET INDUSTRIELS MODERNES
AVRIL PARIS 1925 OCTOBRE

LES ÉDITIONS DE L'IMAGE DE FRANCE
55, rue de Châteaudun, PARIS

1925

The Exposition internationale des arts décoratifs of 1925 focalized the divisions and misunderstandings caused by the term *decorative arts*. In his 1911 report on the international exhibition, Société president René Guilleré pointed out that the Italians had been the first to decide to be "modern" and to exclude imitations of past styles by holding the first special exhibition of modern decorative arts in Turin in 1902. Following the Italian model, the French exhibition thus planned to show exclusively modern art. Roger Marx's proposal, published in 1909, stressed the social role of the decorative arts. Naturally, industry would have an important part to play: "An exhibition of this kind would bring an end to the scorn to which the machine has been subjected; and end the long-standing antagonism between architects and engineers."[1]

In the end, Le Corbusier's *Pavilion de l'Esprit Nouveau* was the only pavilion that corresponded to the original utopian project. There he exposed his *Plan Voisin*, in which the historic centre of Paris was to be replaced by a complex of high-rise buildings.

Le Corbusier had no illusions about the true situation of the decorative arts on this occasion: "If, among the clamour of the crowds, the fireworks and the gilt-plaster palaces, the question of the decorative arts this year seems to have an important place in our preoccupations, it is because 1925 has been exceptionally decreed the year of the 'International Marathon of the Household Arts.'"[2] The year before, in view of this marathon, he had published a series of articles on the decorative arts in *l'Esprit Nouveau*, where he developed his concept of *casiers standards* that would replace traditional furniture, his *human-member objects* that responded to type-needs. "In this International Exhibition of applied arts," he said, "in which everything is to be *particular* and *nothing is to be typical*, it is necessary to try to equip a home with standard furnishings that are designed not for an *art* exhibit or a public accustomed to excess, but for industrial production, and that make no claims to an artistic character within a pretentious decor."[3]

The directors of the Exhibition were quite hostile to the pavilion of *L'Esprit Nouveau* once they finally saw it. It was kept hidden by a six-metre-high fence until its inauguration by the Minister of Education on 10 July 1925.

For Le Corbusier, the decorative arts should be beautiful tools. This was not the view of the authors of most of the prestigious French pavilions, which featured sumptuous interiors like the *Hôtel du collectionneur*, presented by Jacques-Emile Ruhlmann. Critic Leon Deshairs wrote: "We would have been surprised if Ruhlmann had proposed the construction of a worker's house and exhibited cheap

108. *Le Corbusier et Pierre Jeanneret, Pavilion de l'Esprit Nouveau, Exposition des arts décoratifs, 1925.*

furniture."[4] Nor was it the view expressed at the musée d'Art contemporain, where Louis Süe, André Mare, and the Compagnie des arts français, kept "the sense of moderation characteristic of the Latin soul",[5] or in the pavilions by the design studios of the major department stores.

The Société was represented by a lavish ensemble entitled *A French Embassy* that caused an uproar in the press. Gabriel Mourey took the artists to task for "their devotion to the monied powers", and "their lack of comprehension of the demands of modern life".[6] Marie Dormoy gave only reserved praise, after a shattering interview with Auguste Perret, who rejected the decorative arts as a whole: "Where there is true art, there is no need for decoration."[7]

The contemporaries and the moderns divided between themselves the reception rooms and the private apartments. The luxury and calm of the *Woman's Bedroom* by André Groult contrasted with the *Man's Bedroom* by Georges Chevallier and Léon Jallot, "a veritable mortuary

109. A. Levard, Interior of the Pavilion
of the Printemps Department Store,
Exposition des arts décoratifs, 1925.

viewing chamber". Four modern decorators had new ideas that
nevertheless retained elements of luxury and refinement. Pierre
Chareau presented an *Office/Library* with fabrics, carpets and sculptures designed and produced by Hélène Henry, Jean Lurçat and
Jacques Lipschitz. In his *Smoking-room*, Jean Dunand created, according to Marie Dormoy, a "Baudelairean" atmosphere. Francis
Jourdain used simplicity and plainness in his *Physical culture room*
and the *Smoking-room*: "You can decorate a room very luxuriously by
unfurnishing it rather than by furnishing it."[8] Finally, Robert Mallet-
Stevens employed clear, elegant geometry in a decor enlivened by a
bas-relief by Henri Laurens and paintings by Fernand Léger and Robert
Delaunay.
All forms of decorative arts were displayed in the French and foreign
pavilions, and in the galleries of the Grand Palais. Here were sheltered
decorative arts in all varieties—traditional and modern, handcrafted
and industrial. Divisions end when reality and utopia coexist.

Yvonne Brunhammer

1925

110. View of the Exposition des arts décoratifs, 1925. Autochrome. Boulogne, Collections Albert Kahn. Right: pavilion of the department store A la Place Clichy. In background, pavilion of the Bon Marché department store.

In 1912, the Commission of Commerce and Industry of the French Chamber of Deputies ratified a project for an international exhibition of modern decorative and industrial arts to be held in Paris in 1915, claiming that the exhibition was necessary for the defence of national interests—both artistic and economic—and that it should be considered an urgent obligation by the Republic.[1] Unlike the Paris Universal Expositions that had preceded it, this specialized exhibition was aimed at finding solutions to a broad range of problems experienced by French art industries since the mid-nineteenth century, when the machine and the division of labour were introduced into craft production.[2] The issues at stake,

however, were not only artistic and economic, but also cultural and nationalistic: the luxury crafts had always been considered one of the nation's traditional sources of prestige. Sponsored by the Ministry of Commerce and the Ministry of Fine Arts, it was a broad-based effort to foster progress in industry and to generate a French style for the twentieth century. The most striking aspect of the programme was the stipulation that everything in the exhibition had to be "modern", and that the definition and promotion of modernity would be effected by official institution. It attempted to address the crisis situation in the nation's decorative arts industries, which revolved around methods of

professional training, the problem of historicism, and the nonexistence of a professional relationship between artists, artisans, and manufacturers. Involving almost all sectors of French industry, it would channel dispersed efforts to modernize decorative arts production into a unified programme of action.

At the same time, the project also attempted to address a more general and difficult problem regarding the national economy. France was the world leader in luxury commerce: its industry leaned heavily towards expensive manufactures of higher-quality finish and design and could not compete with more industrially-developed nations like England and Germany in the production of inexpensive, standardized goods.[3] Those who developed the first exhibition project were convinced that through the application of art to all branches of industry, the exhibition would lead manufacturers to a more standard production for everyday use possessing the same qualities of design and refinement as luxury goods. The democratization of society would provide a market for which industry could provide the means: good design could be made available to all classes of society.

Knowing how it turned out when it was finally realized in 1925, it is difficult to imagine that the exhibition began with an ideology of an "art for the people". The first suggestion for the international exhibition of decorative arts was made in the Chamber of Deputies in 1906 by the Radical-Socialist Charles Couyba (1866-1931), a supporter of the Société, as part of his annual project for the budget of the Administration of Fine Arts.[4] He stressed the importance of the reform of the decorative arts, especially in light of the recent projects for workers' housing and Habitations à bon marché (inexpensive housing projects) that were developing over the

past few years. For these, inexpensive and aesthetically pleasing furnishings were required—art, science and mechanization, he insisted, should respond to these new needs: "Our artists must be encouraged on the path towards a practical and popular decor." An international exhibition of decorative arts, Couyba suggested, would foster new research and encourage artists and manufacturers to provide designs for unlimited production which all classes of society could use.

Couyba's project was taken up by

Roger Marx, eminent art critic, advocate of decorative arts reform, and Inspector of Provincial Museums. In 1909, he published an article entitled "On social art and the necessity of ensuring its progress by an exhibition", in which he explained that the decorative arts epitomized the notion of an "art for the people" or "social art".[5] Intimately linked to the individual as well as to the community, the decorative arts knew no class distinctions; they addressed questions of aesthetics, sociology and political economy. Roger Marx's views were certainly influenced by those of the English reformers John Ruskin and William Morris, but he realized that non-mechanized craft production was utopian in an age of competitive world markets, and he encouraged artists to accept the machine. Only then could it gain its rightful place as an indispensable tool in the dissemination and democratization of beauty. Mass production, Roger Marx explained, could ensure the victory of good taste and modern design, and allow France to conquer larger

1925

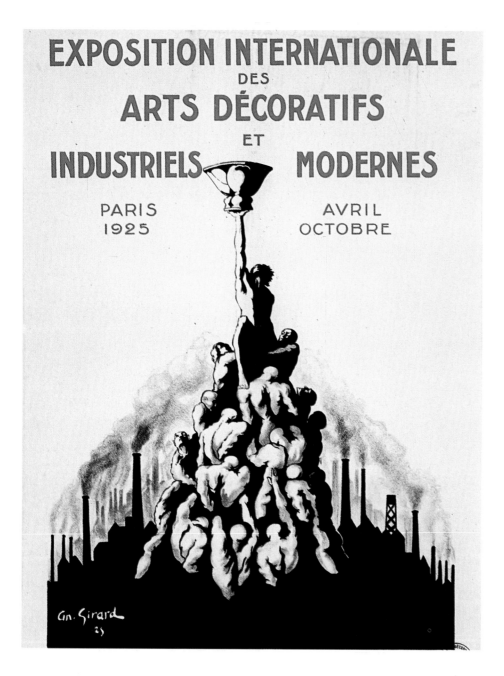

113. A. Girard, Poster for the Exposition des arts décoratifs, *1925, musée de la Publicité.*

114. René Lalique, Illuminated fountain located in front of the Cour des métiers, *Exposition des arts décoratifs, 1925.*

export markets. He proposed that the government plan an exhibition in which there would be no question of repeating the encyclopaedic and often disorganized Universal Expositions of the past; it could be effective only if it had a clearly defined theme. And most important, like the first international exhibition of decorative arts in Turin in 1902, the exhibition programme would include only those works that could be defined as specifically new:

> We would also like it to be modern, that all reminiscence of the past be mercilessly excluded from it, the inventions of social art having an interest or purpose only insofar as they rigorously adapt themselves to the times which bring them into being.

The Société des artistes décorateurs had begun discussing the need for a decorative arts exhibition in December 1910, when member Charles Hairon suggested that it take the initiative to push the project, using official reports on the national economy to demonstrate the importance of decorative arts to French commerce.[6] It was then that René Guilleré, in collaboration with representatives of the Société, the Salon d'Automne and the Société d'encouragement à l'art et à l'industrie, began preparing the official report on the exhibition that he submitted to the Chamber of Deputies in 1911.[7] By the time the project was formulated in Guilleré's report, however, it had already lost its proposition for an "art social". The project, now of vast dimensions, was defined as follows:

> To assemble in an international exhibition—through a collaboration between the artist, the industrialist and the artisan—all of the decorative arts: architecture, woodcrafts, stone and metal work, ceramics, glass, paper and fabrics, etc., in all of their forms, be they applied to useful objects or to purely decorative

works; in all of their destinations: exterior and interior decoration of public and private buildings, furniture, personal adornment. . . . This must be an exhibition of Modern Art exclusively. No copy or pastiche of old styles will be admitted.[8]

François Carnot, Deputy, and president of the Union centrale des arts décoratifs, prepared the draft proposal for the Exhibition projected for 1915; it was ratified by the Chamber on 12 July 1912.[9] Carnot was placed at the head of the commission charged with studying the programme, and he stipulated that acceptance in the exposition would be based on the modernity of the work presented, and not on the reputation of the artist or manufacturer. Most important, he developed a new concept in the organization and presentation of works. They would not be piled up in individual stands as in past expositions, but presented in realistic ensembles showing how they could function in daily life:

> The modern decorative arts, in all of their forms, must be presented as a living reality, fully appropriate to present-day needs, aesthetic as well as material, and not as the chance assembly of a large number of objects for shopwindow displays, all different and without any particular destination. A ceramic tile, a wallpaper or fabric take on their meaning only on the surface which they are supposed to decorate. A desk has value only in the context of the office for which it is destined; a desk lamp is justified only on the desk which it is supposed to light; in a word, to make the modern decorative arts be understood and to give a clear feeling of their existence and their specific value, each object presented must participate, insofar as it is possible, in the logical constitution of a homogenous ensemble.[10]

To achieve this, Carnot suggested that the objects be shown in context through the construction of individual houses, villas, and hotels, model workers' accomodations and their furnishings, as well as cafés, restaurants, post offices, and schools; in effect, in the form of an ideal city of the future.[11] The project, however, met with considerable opposition from sectors of the industrial community which contested the prerogative of the government to decide what was "modern" and what was not. It meant, of course, that all those manufacturers specialized in copies of historical styles would be excluded.[12] Squabbling among the various interest groups likely to be involved in the exhibition brought the project to a standstill in 1913, and the advent of the war ended all discussion for the next four years.

The project was resumed in July 1919 as part of the post-war programme of industrial development and economic recovery, in a climate of drastic economic fluctuations, inflation and currency depreciation.[13] The government and the artistic and industrial communities placed high hopes on the exhibition, projected for 1923 (later postponed until 1925), and saw it as the starting point for an "artistic, industrial and commercial renaissance".[14] By the beginning of 1923, manufacturing and commercial milieux, recognizing the importance of the project, had organized themselves to take a leading role in the direction of the exhibition, and had even raised 3.5 million francs in subsidies.[15]

Although the Société had been one of the principal engineers behind the original project for the exhibition, much to its surprise and disappointment the new administration did not ask the Société to play the leading role it thought it deserved. And since no subsidies were to be awarded for its participation in the exhibition, it seemed that the Société might not be

able to exhibit as a group at all. In October 1923, the committee sent an official letter of protest to Paul Léon, Director of Fine Arts, and even considered encouraging individual members to boycott the exhibition entirely. Finally, in March 1924, after a long series of negotiations, the administration granted funds for the construction of a pavilion for a group presentation—but only on the condition that it have a coherent theme, in accordance with the exhibition rules laid out by François Carnot. Even with the subsidies, however, the individual artist members still had no funds to create the works they would display. The Société first considered solving this problem through the creation of a consortium of "rich art lovers" who would finance individual works—those unsold at the exhibition's end would become the property of the consortium.[16] When they were unable to realize this project, the Ministry of Fine Arts stepped in with a solution. It offered to finance an ensemble of interiors intended for a French Embassy, which would permit a broad sector of the members of the Société to participate. After the exhibition, the state would become the owner of all unsold works for which it had given funds.[17]

The Paris Exposition internationale des arts décoratifs et industriels modernes was inaugurated by the President of the Republic on 28 April 1925. The "Reception Rooms and Private Apartments of an Embassy" by the Société were located in the galleries of the *Cour des métiers* designed by Charles Plumet, on the Esplanade des Invalides at the head of the central axis of the Exhibition. To accommodate all the branches of decorative arts included in the Société the presentation was divided into four sections: reception rooms, private apartments for important ensembles, and an art gallery and a collection hall for small art objects and decorative sculpture. All the exhibits were the result of a collaborative effort, and a broad range of styles was represented: works produced by luxury craftsmanship as well as by the workshops of the Parisian department

116. La Cour des métiers. *Fountain by Pierre-Marie Poisson, vases by Jean Dunand, decorative murals representing the arts and industries.*

stores. Among the most successful in the section devoted to reception rooms was the *Grand salon de réception* put together by Henri Rapin and Pierre Selmersheim. An astounding variety of decorative art works co-existed here: sculpted bas-relief friezes by Henri Bouchard and Gaston Le Bourgeois; a large decorative painting, *La Danse*, by Gustave Jaulmes; silk wall hangings including *Les jets d'eau*, and a carpet executed by Aubusson, all designed by Edouard Benedictus; furnishings in wrought iron by Edgar Brandt; a grand piano by Louis Süe and

117. *Jean Dunand,* Vases exhibited in the Cour des métiers. *Copper lacquered black with silver inlays.*

André Mare; and numerous examples of fine cabinetwork by Fernand Nathan, Léon Bouchet, Léon Jallot, and Pierre Montagnac. The interior was further embellished by small *objets d'art* such as copper vases by Claudius Linossier, coffers in ivory and mother-of-pearl by Georges Bastard, ceramics by Henri Simmen, and decorative sculptures by Charles Despiau and Joseph Bernard. The *Dining-room* by Henri Rapin, however, cast doubt among critics about the Société's am-

bition to create a modern style. The monumental space was covered by a barrel-vault made of decorated glass panels. The end walls were surmounted by two tympana containing stylized, neo-classical bas-reliefs by Max Blondat on the themes "The Arrival of the Ambassador" and "The Presentation of Diplomatic Credentials".

The black-lacquer *Smoking-room* by Jean Dunand was one of the most unusual and admired interiors. Displaying a table and four armchairs

118. Henri Rapin et Pierre Selmersheim, Grand Salon *of the* French Embassy.

119. Claudius Linossier, Vases.
Hammered copper encrusted with silver.

120. Edouard Benedictus, Les jets d'eau,
Edged satin. Paris, musée des Arts décoratifs.

121. *Henri Rapin,* Dining-room.

122. *Jean Dunand,* Smoking-room.

Following double page:
123. *Jean Dunand,* Smoking-room.

designed in a decorative Cubist style, it dazzled by its new conception of space, as complex as a Chinese puzzle: the silver ceiling with touches of red lacquer ascended in ziggurat-form on four levels; the corners of the room were bevelled, reveted in black-lacquered panels, and flanked by tri-angular pilasters; a divan with var-nished leather cushions was placed within an alcove that formed part of the room's geometrical composition.

In the private apartments, it was the *Woman's Bedroom* by André Groult that attracted unanimous praise. Groult took a painterly approach to the interior, harmonizing pastel tones and sinuous, almost feminine lines. His curving, voluptuous furnishings, sheathed in beige-grey sharkskin

(*galuchat*), and his "anthropomorphic" *chiffonier* contrasted sharply with the geometric aesthetic so prevalent throughout the exhibition. The ensemble was finished with draperies in rose-coloured silk, and portraits in oil and watercolour by Marie Laurencin. The sober *Man's Bedroom* by Léon Jallot and Georges Chevallier seemed lackluster in comparison, leading one critic to ask if the ambassador who was to sleep there was a "morose old man".[18] The ensemble was enlivened, however, by the geometric lamps of Jean Perzel. The four grouped interiors by Pierre Chareau, Robert Mallet-Stevens and Francis Jourdain augured a new aesthetic. The *Office/Library* in palmwood by Chareau had a bold, circular structure with walls that could be opened or closed to create a private space around the desk, topped by a cupola that diffused artificial light. Built-in bookcases created an open and

126. Jean Perzel, Lamp *shown in the* Man's Bedroom *by Léon Jallot and Georges Chevalier.*

124. André Groult, Chiffonier, *shown in his* Woman's Bedroom. *Shagreen.*

125. André Groult, Woman's Bedroom.

Right page:

127. Léon Jallot and Georges Chevalier, Man's Bedroom.

128. *Pierre Chareau,* Office/Library.

uncluttered space. The room barely contained any decoration, only a sculpture by Jacques Lipschitz. The adjoining *Smoking-room* by Francis Jourdain was an exploration of spatial economy. The small interior was painted bright yellow and also contained built-in bookcases as well as cabinets and seats. The only free-standing furniture consisted of two geometric armchairs and a small round table, Jourdain collaborated with Chareau on the adjoining *Physical culture room* and

Lounge. In Jourdain's *Physical culture room,* the walls were covered with large plaques of wood attached with tacks to imitate riveted metal. Chareau's *Lounge* contained a suspended bed resembling the one that he had created for the Villa de Noailles at Hyères. The bold geometric fabrics were designed by Helène Henry, while Sonia Delaunay contributed a pyjama and bathrobe made of what she called "simultaneous" fabric, designed with colourful motifs. The *Hall*

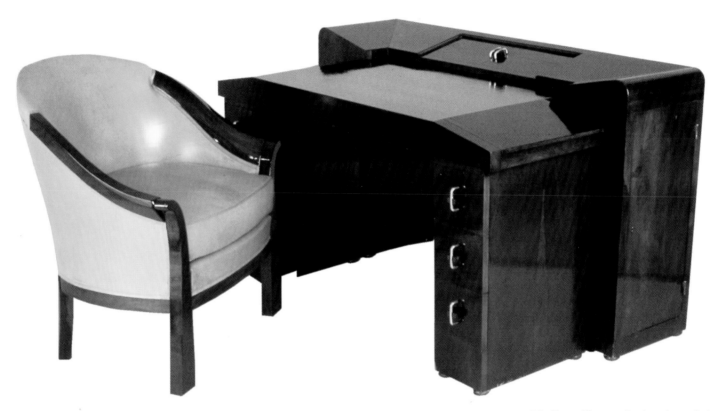

129. *Pierre Chareau,* Desk and armchair *shown in the Office/Library. Palisander verneer, oak and mahogany. Paris, musée des Arts décoratifs.*

130. *Pierre Chareau,* Office/Library. *Walls in palmwood.*

131. *Francis Jourdain,* Smoking-room.

133. *Francis Jourdain,* Physical culture room.
In background, Lounge *by Pierre Chareau.*

132. *Francis Jourdain,* Smoking-room.

134. *Francis Jourdain,* Physical culture room.

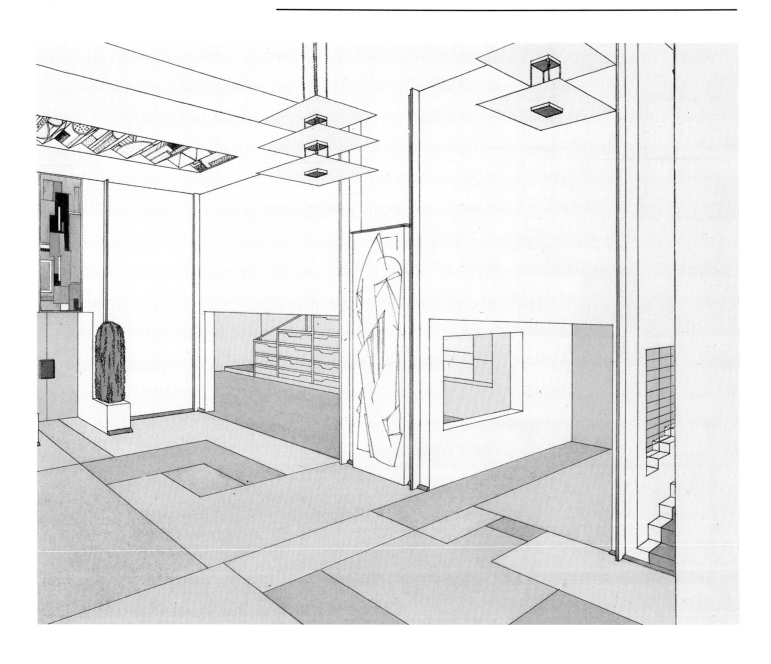

135. *Robert Mallet-Stevens*, Hall.

and Winter Garden by Mallet-Stevens had attracted the attention and sympathy of the press even before the exhibition opened when, just before the inauguration, the Société's committee asked the architect to remove the Cubist paintings by Robert Delaunay and Fernand Léger that formed part of the ensemble. After an outcry from the press, the paintings remained, providing coloured accents for Mallet-Stevens' stark, controlled geometry.

The Exposition des arts décoratifs and the presentation by the Société were an enormous success in France and abroad. The exhibition launched the French *Moderne* throughout Europe and especially in the United States, where a large number of works, among them many presented in the Société's apartments for the French Embassy,

were sent on a travelling exhibition in 1926.

The Société had finally won the recognition for modern decorative arts that it had been seeking for twenty-five years, but meanwhile it had lost sight of its goal of making the arts available to everyone. Although most of the individual works displayed were of the highest artistic and technical quality, few of the interiors could genuinely be described as "total works of art", and even fewer suggested a new way of life possible through the spiritual liberation supposedly offered by the arrival of mechanization—the stated goal of the exhibition project. Those who remembered the original ideals of the exhibition proclaimed from 1906 to 1911 were profoundly disappointed. The exhibition unleashed a storm of criticism that would have been unthinkable only a few months earlier. For Francis Jourdain, who had fought for the ideals of an "art for the people" since the beginning of his career, the exhibition was a failure that had provided no genuine solution to the real problems of modern domestic furnishing:

> This exhibition is inconsequent. It has no meaning, it teaches no lesson, and it resolves no problem. It has not even posed one. At the most it has permitted us to meditate upon the problem of figuring out if the fruit basket constitutes a more "modern" ornament than the chestnut leaf of 1900, or if the great ornamental conquest of the period was not in fact, the fan shape. I admit to being one of those whose sleep is not troubled by such solutions.[19]

The critic Gabriel Mourey, who had been following the decorative arts reform movement since the 1890s, was of the same opinion. He wrote in *L'Amour de l'Art* that the exhibition had been almost entirely devoted to

136. Robert Delaunay, La Femme et La Tour, *shown in the* Hall *by Robert Mallet-Stevens.*

138. Jean Dupas, Les Perruches *in the* Hôtel
du collectionneur *by Jacques-Emile Ruhlmann.*
Exposition des arts décoratifs. *1925.*
Autochrome. Boulogne, collections Albert Kahn.

137. Jacques-Emile Ruhlmann,
Petit Salon *in the* Hôtel du collectionneur,
Exposition des arts décoratifs, *Autochrome.*
Boulogne, Collections Albert Kahn.

luxury goods and that the entire concept was immoral and anti-social, especially since the French economy had not yet recovered from the war:

It is not the Exhibition, but modern decorative arts that are anti-social and anti-democratic. Modern decorative arts, which are essentially conservative and retrograde, do not give a fig, or seem not to give a fig, for the popular clientele. They do not understand its needs. They produce for the rich. . . . The French and foreign designers work only for the privileged class. To have named an ensemble, as Ruhlmann did: "Townhouse of a Rich Collector", displays either a completely cynical spirit or a rare insensitivity. False luxury is in fact the dominant note of the entire exhibition. . . . In choosing an Embassy as a theme rather than a People's Centre, the Société des artistes décorateurs has given ample proof of the spirit in which our architects, furniture makers and decorators work. And these architects and furniture-makers are reactionary not only by their devotion to the 'powers of wealth', but also by their lack of comprehension of the needs imposed by modern life.[20]

From another point of view, the exhibition achieved part of what its planners wanted: to find new applications for a wide range of traditional luxury crafts, to reestablish Paris as the world centre of style and taste, and to create a new and uniquely French style of

decorative arts that rivalled those of the past. In any case, the Société's contribution provided an important forum for the confrontation of two fundamentally different approaches to the interior—that proposed by Mallet-Stevens, Chareau and Jourdain, and that of Rapin, Selmersheim, Jallot, and others. While all of the interiors were essentially luxurious, the presentation by Chareau, Jourdain and Mallet-Stevens addressed more modern concepts of space—concepts that would gain in importance after 1925. For these designers the interior was not a theatre in which dramatic objects could be presented, but rather, space was appreciated for its inherent aesthetic qualities, and each piece in it was considered in relation to the whole, uncluttered by unnecessary details.

Perhaps this was the first sign of modernity in the French interior. As a writer for *Les Arts de la Maison* observed:

> It will be the glory of the 1925 Exhibition to have stretched ornamentation to its limits, to the point of having turned young designers from it and pushed them towards a search for form and volume which ornamentation had eclipsed. . . . Architecture, which is only in the first stages of its renewal, will solve the problem of interior arrangement which is so poorly posed today. . . . It will replace the decorative role played by furniture by enlivening the walls with just a few fine canvases. It will be healthy, convenient, practical. And above all, it will be beautiful. . . . [21]

Suzanne Tise

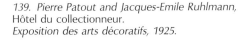

139. Pierre Patout and Jacques-Emile Ruhlmann,
Hôtel du collectionneur.
Exposition des arts décoratifs, 1925.

*140. Louis Süe and André Mare,
Salle des fêtes installed in the Grand Palais,
Exposition des arts décoratifs, 1925.*

1925

141. *Henri Sauvage*, Gallery of Boutiques,
Exposition des arts décoratifs, 1925.
Autochrome. Boulogne, collections Albert Kahn.

142. Robert Mallet-Stevens and Jan
and Joël Martel, Cubist Garden.
Clothing and accessories by Sonia Delaunay.
Exposition des arts décoratifs, 1925.

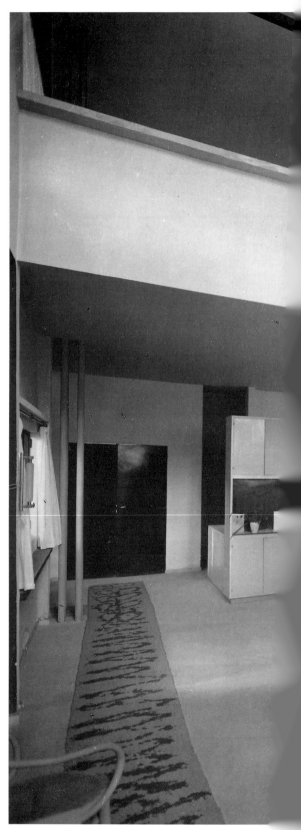

143. Le Corbusier and Pierre Jeanneret,
Pavilion de l'Esprit Nouveau.
Exposition des arts décoratifs, 1925.

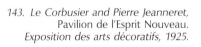

1926-1929

Between 1926 and 1929 the activities of the Société des artistes décorateurs were marked by conflicts between tradition and the avant-garde, art versus industry, and the defenders versus the adversaries of ornamentation. The conflicts resulted in the departure of nearly thirty members who in 1929 founded an association of their own, the Union des artistes modernes (UAM). The 1925 Exhibition had exemplified the Société's divisions, and the break between the upholders of tradition and those of modernity was a recurring one in the decorative arts.

From the start, in spite of its contradictory declarations, the Société consistently took the side of luxury goods rather than functional objects. The success, even triumph, of the 1925 Exhibition sprang from its conspicuous display of luxury, and the Salon of the following year confirmed this direction. In his preface to the Salon's catalogue, Fernand David, who had been chief commissioner of the Exposition des arts décoratifs, justified this choice in the name of "a close bond with real life". Indeed, the artists could not disappoint their traditional clientele.

Nevertheless, next to the baroque ornamental exuberance a new tendency appeared that brought the decorative tradition to the fringes of the modern movement. While not breaking away from the principle of unique, handmade pieces and fine furniture, it did turn towards decorative abstraction through geometricized Art Deco.

The furnishings for Jacques Doucet's studio in Neuilly were the final, sublime point that Art Deco would reach in its abstract phase. The decorators chosen by the couturier in 1923 had to harmonize their designs with a collection that included Cubist and Surrealist paintings and art objects. The pure, geometric, detailed work by Pierre Legrain, Marcel Coard, and the carpets designed by the sculptors Gustave Miklos and Joseph Csaky, all used, to some extent, precious materials like exotic wood, lacquer, parchment, and ivory.

Jacques-Emile Ruhlmann represented better than anyone an evolution that, just before his death in 1933, led him to adopt such materials as metal and glass. Though remaining entirely loyal to his clientele, and thus to the luxury object, he intensified the classical aspect of furniture that had become apparent since 1919. His *meuble d'appui* for the *Hôtel du collectionneur* in 1925 was a milestone: its doors sported animal figures painted by Jean Lambert-Rucki on a black lacquer background, flanked by fluted pilasters in the style of Josef Hoffmann. The geometric, unadorned office furniture Ruhlmann designed between 1932 and 1933 for the Maharajah of Indore was the culmination of this classical wave, a move away from the eighteenth-century-style elegance of the tapered furniture legs and floral marquetry that had made the fame of cabinetmakers in the 1920s.

1926-1929

144. *Jean Dunand,* Detail of the Portrait of Madame Agnès, *shown in the* Study for an Art Collector *by Jacques-Emile Ruhlmann, Salon of the Société des artistes décorateurs, 1926 (see fig. 170).*

145. *Le Corbusier, Pierre Jeanneret, and Charlotte Perriand,* Siège tournant *shown in the* Dining-room *by Charlotte Perriand, 1928. Chromed tubular steel and leather. musée des Arts décoratifs, Paris.*

146. *Charlotte Perriand,* Dining room, *Salon of the Société des artistes décorateurs, 1928.*

Whether or not they renounced ornamentation, the artistes décorateurs depended on a three-way production system that consisted of a client, a designer and a craftsman. This system was contested by the European avant-garde, and in France by the founders of the UAM, who derided the current social need to use industry for mass production, reducing the role of the artiste décorateur to that of a designer of models. Already in 1925, despite homage to the crafts tradition on which all industrial creation must be based, the Bauhaus proposed furniture and objects that required materials more appropriate to industrial production: metal and glass. Although the Bauhaus did not participate in the 1925 Exhibition, the furniture designed that year by Marcel Breuer—particularly the *Vassily* chair, its leather or cloth stretched over a visible metal frame—undoubtedly played a part in the appearance of the metal tube at the Salon of the artistes décorateurs in 1928. Still, fundamental questions were not being raised and objects continued to be viewed from the standpoint of decoration. It was not by replacing cornucopias and flowers with triangles that the much-needed revolution in furniture would take place: "Caprice disguised as geometry", wrote the critic Léon Werth, after the Salon of 1927.[1] The temptation of ornament struck even the painters of the De Stijl movement. Pure painting and abstract painting, it seemed, were converging with decoration.

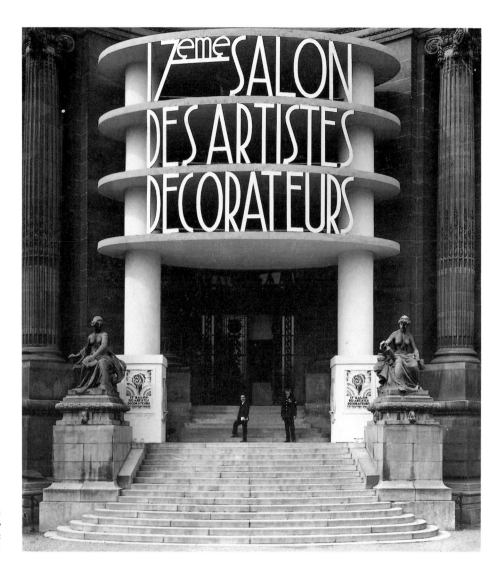

147. Gabriel Englinger, Main Entrance designed for the 17th Salon of the Société des artistes décorateurs at the Grand Palais, 1927.

The 1920s ended with the New York stock market crash. And yet not since the end of the First World War had France known such prosperity. No one would have believed that the crisis could ever extend as far as France. New social legislation that had been voted the previous year was applied in 1929, specifically social security and the Loucheur Law on the construction of inexpensive housing. This law had a decisive effect on French architecture, and especially on homes and furnishings. The avant-garde that formed at the Salon of 1928 around Charlotte Perriand, Djo Bourgeois and René Herbst, tried to respond to this opportunity by creating the Union des artistes modernes dedicated to "Modern Art, the decor for contemporary life". The president of the Société in 1929 was André Tardieu, also the Député of the Territoire-de-Belfort, or Belfort-Campagne, where the wealthy upper class lived. That same year, he was appointed *Président du conseil*, and he dominated French politics until 1932. His official support clearly showed the course that the Société des artistes décorateurs meant to follow. The subsequent Société-UAM split was caused by ideological differences, political as well as aesthetic.

Yvonne Brunhammer

123

1926-1929

The sixteenth Salon of the Société des artistes décorateurs opened at the Grand Palais little more than six months after the closing of the 1925 Exposition. Criticism of the Exhibition apparently provoked dissatisfaction within the Société membership, because more than fifteen of the most established artists, among them Mallet-Stevens, Francis Jourdain, René Gabriel and René Prou, abstained from the 1926 Salon. Many members of the Société participated in an alternative exhibition organized by Henri Clouzot at the Musée Galliera in January of that year devoted to the theme "Furniture for the average French family", an exhibit that was an "indirect critique of the initiators of the International Exhibition of Decorative Arts who did not have preoccupations of a practical nature".[1] Fernand David, who had been Chief Commissioner of the International Exhibition, was invited to preface the Société's 1926 catalogue, and he proclaimed that the Salon of that year marked a new direction for the association. He defended the Société to critics who had condemned its lack of attention to the needs of the average person by insisting that the public would never have been won over to modern design if the designers had presented only ordinary objects:

> What the designers discovered there is worth pointing out: the necessity for close contact with real life. They were reproached with having created mostly exceptional designs, rare pieces; a reproach, by the way, that was not entirely founded, for many exhibitors showed interesting work for mass production. But it should be kept in mind that the designers work for an aristocratic clientele. Furthermore, given the exceptional nature of the exhibition, the exhibitors displayed a kind of politeness in choosing their most magnificent designs to submit to the world's consideration. . . . The aim of the exhibition, which was to bring out the artistic qualities of everyday objects as well as those of luxury items, may have been somewhat subverted as a result. Should this be regretted? What interests the public is the diversity of designs as much as their luxuriousness. The exhibition might not have been a triumph had it brought together only objects of everyday use. . . .[2]

124

148. *Michel Roux-Spitz, Central Rotunda, 1926 Salon.*

David went on to explain that a new contact with "real life" would lead the designers in 1926 to turn their attention to the needs of the "average French person". But the entries proved that nothing was further from the truth. The sumptuous interiors of the preceding year had taken a turn for the baroque and were overpowered by geometric and floral motifs on upholstery, wallcoverings and carpets. Maurice Dufrène exhibited a series of interiors destined for "the ordinary Frenchman" that sold for the extravagant sum of 100,000 francs.[3] For the critic Yvanhoé Rambosson, the artists were totally unaware that the real success of 1925 had been in the enthusiasm it generated for modern design. The artists had created desires that they were not prepared to satisfy. What was needed, he insisted, was the immediate ad-

149. Paul Follot, Vestibule, 1926.
Designed for La Pomone.

with a decor that corresponds to the evolution of their vision. They will be satisfied only through mass-produced fabrications, which have been studied equally closely from the economic and from the artistic points of view.[4]

One interior that attracted the whole-hearted praise of critics, however, was the *Chambre à la campagne* (bedroom for a country house) exhibited by the architect Georges Djo-Bourgeois (1898-1937), who had been a student of Mallet-Stevens at the Ecole spéciale d'architecture. His interior displayed little that was rustic, however, and was sparsely furnished with a built-in bed, corner desk, and large armchair. The most striking aspect of his presentation was his attempt to create the experience of total space. He combined architecture and furnishings harmoniously; the furniture was simple and rigidly geometric and colour applied to furniture, floors and walls unified the room. The plane surfaces and terminal edges of the furniture were defined with different colours —yellow, light brown and cream white. The floor and the walls were painted with floating squares of beige, ochre and black—further serving to unite the architecture and the furnishings.

Simplicity and rationalism in French design, first introduced in 1925 by the team of Chareau, Mallet-Stevens and Jourdain, and continued by Djo-Bourgeois in 1926, marked for the first time the beginning of a pronounced stylistic division among the members of the Société. Ernest Tisserand, writing in *L'Art Vivant*, observed the number of abstentions in the Salon and remarked that there were grave problems in the Société's direction. He predicted an imminent mutiny within the ranks:

> There is no need to be a great prophet to sense the air of dissent that floats in the north wing of the Grand Palais. Next year we will per-

aptation of the luxurious models exhibited in 1925 to serial production to meet the demand of the middle classes who wanted to decorate their homes with modern furnishings, but in the present circumstances, could not afford them:

> The designs of our artists appealed to people through wonderful works, one-of-a-kind pieces, whose acquisition is accessible only to the few. Admiration, however, is not enough for those who have been won over by the new aspect of this art. There are more and more people of taste who wish to surround themselves

haps visit the first Salon of Independent Designers. In art, division is a strength.[5]

The 1927 Salon showed little willingness on the part of the artists to abandon the stylish luxury that had been so successful in 1925 for practical furnishings that would bring modern design to a broader audience. The Salon of 1928, however, demonstrated a move towards more innovative materials and an international aesthetic. Fifteen members showed rooms containing some furnishings that were being reproduced in more than one copy, but the major change was the appearance of furniture in tubular and sheet steel. This was undoubtedly the result of the Die Wohnung exhibition held in Stuttgart the previous year that featured tubular

150. Djo-Bourgeois, Bedroom for Villa on the Côte d'Azur, *1926.*

151. Maurice Dufrène, Study, 1926. Carpet by Suzanne Guiguichon, small secretary by Gabriel Englinger. Designed for La Maîtrise.

1926-1929

152. René Lalique, Vase, 1927.
Amber glass. Paris, galerie Bramy.

steel furnishings by Bauhaus artist Marcel Breuer, and that had been widely covered in architecture and decoration reviews in France.[6] The Parisian department stores were quick to join this trend. Maurice Dufrène's interior design for a country house produced by La Maîtrise (Galeries Lafayette), contained several chair models in tubular steel; Maurice Matet, in the *Woman's Study* created for Studium (Louvre), also employed tubular steel chairs which he covered with comfortable pigskin cushions that almost entirely masked their structure.

Lucie Holt le Son, one of only three women contributing entire ensembles to the Salon, designed a *Travel Agency* in which the furnishings were made of lacquered sheet steel and thin plaques of cement. The walls were painted with bold Cubist-inspired murals representing travel by land, air, and sea.

The most successful steel furnishings were found in a group presentation: a model apartment by Charlotte-Perriand, Djo-Bourgeois and René Herbst. Djo-Bourgeois' two-storey Salon was executed in plaster, but was certainly intended for reinforced con-

153. Lucie Holt Le Son, Travel Agency, 1928.

crete. Its bold geometric composition included a projecting mezzanine and staircase that descended to form the structure for a built-in divan. His interior was entirely devoid of decorative additions, and he presented no paintings or sculpture; he preferred instead to rely on the play of architectural forms in space and the printed fabrics designed by his wife, Elise George. He explained his approach in an interview in 1928:

> Being an enemy of unnecessary and decorative complications, I seek simplicity and harmony of volume and colour. The arrangement of a room should form a whole in which no single object should have a pre-ponderant place. The ensemble should be homogenous and form a frame for private life. Unity does not mean monotony or dismalness, and I try to achieve warmth and gay colour schemes.[7]

Djo-Bourgeois' installation included two display cases containing jewellery by Jean Fouquet, who also exhibited a mechanistic *Vanity Box for a Scientific Age*, in gold, and a selection of enamel cigarette cases by Gerard Sandoz.

Djo-Bourgeois' salon opened onto the *Smoking-room* by René Herbst, an architect and designer who had revolutionized the art of window display and merchandise presentation through his work for the Maison Siègel in Paris. His

154. Maurice Dufrène, Interior for a Country House, 1928. Designed for La Maîtrise.

155. François Decorchemont,
Bowl, 1927. Paris,
Félix Marcilhac Collection.

display featured two elegant *chaises longues* in tubular steel, and a floor lamp in chromed steel and aluminium that reflected a vertical beam of light from a steel disk. The most successful of the three interiors was the *Dining-room* designed by Charlotte Perriand. A student of Henri Rapin at the Ecole des arts décoratifs and of Maurice Dufrène in courses at La Maîtrise, she had been exhibiting at the Société since 1926, and had entered Le Corbusier's firm in October 1927. Her style in 1928 exhibited a dramatic change from that of the 1927 Salon. The dining-room was furnished with the telescoping *table extensible* that could be closed to one-third of its length to save space. The four *sièges*

tournants in chromed tubular steel were covered with coral red leather. Jean Puiforcat contributed the simple silverware on the table.

Response by critics to the installations by Herbst, Perriand and Djo-Bourgeois was extremely enthusiastic: they were called the new avant-garde, "daring young spirits always forging ahead", and who had emerged next to "a majority of less adventuresome talents, who preserve the result achieved in the course of the years, while assimilating all they can from the initiatives of the avant-garde".[8]

Their success in 1928 led them to plan an even larger group exhibit for the Salon of 1929. This time Pierre Chareau and Mallet-Stevens were in charge of developing the overall scheme of the installation. Charlotte Perriand planned to present the prototypes for the *Equipement d'habitation* (later manufactured by Thonet) that she had designed in collaboration with Le Corbusier and Pierre Jeanneret. The jury of the Salon, however, rejecting the idea of an extended group exhibit, refused to accord a space large enough to accommodate them. As a result, Herbst and Perriand resigned from the Société, soon followed by sixteen other members, including Francis Jourdain, Mallet-Stevens, Jean Fouquet, Jan and Joel Martel and Gerard Sandoz. The resignations caused an uproar in the Société. There were accusations of corruption, in particular by Maurice Dufrène, who staunchly defended the right of the group to exhibit freely even though he himself was not among them. Dufrène accused the committee of dishonest practices and of abandoning the Société's original ideals. Vice-president Charles Hairon countered with the claim that the group had been refused simply because the artists were too slow turning in their plans for the Salon, and the jury had no choice but to give their space to another designer.[9] But according to Perriand, the committee had been looking for any reason to exclude the group from the Société because they had attracted too much attention at the previous year's Salon:

> We had a great success. People spoke of the group that had emerged from the *Décorateurs*, of this faction emerging from the run-of-the-mill. And when, with Le Corbusier, we wanted to hold our exhibition in 1929, I asked the *Décorateurs* for a group space with the same ones [Herbst, etc.] but they refused. They refused, saying that it would be a Salon within a Salon. Which was somewhat true, as a matter of fact.[10]

And when Djo-Bourgeois was interviewed by *L'Art Vivant* about the incident he explained:

> I did not exhibit at the *Décorateurs*. We wanted to form a group with Mallet-Stevens, Chareau, Jourdain, Herbst, Le Corbusier, Charlotte Perriand, and others, to create an ensemble that would break away from the monotonous individual boxes so dear to the principles of the Société. But no agreement could be reached within the Société itself. We therefore preferred to abstain, all of us. We were about twenty of the same persuasion. This would please a few, and the Salon would be more homogenous.[11]

In May, during the 1929 Salon, the "dissidents" announced the formation of the Union des artistes modernes.[12] As Charlotte Perriand later described it, they "were going to form a group

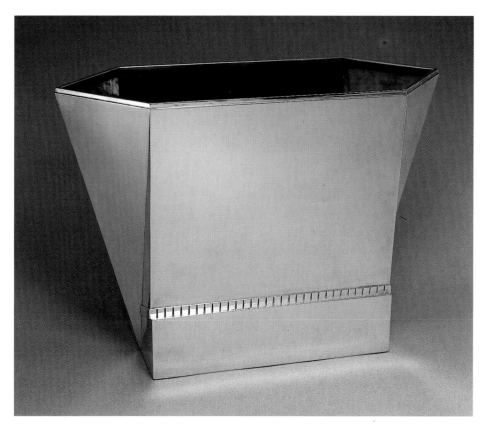

156. Jean Puiforcat, Hexagonal vase, 1927 Salon. Solid silver. Paris, galerie Suger.

that included all fields: architecture, town planning, interior design—taking away the word 'designer' of course".[13] In the first statement published by the UAM, Francis Jourdain explained why it had become impossible for him and his colleagues to continue to exhibit with the Société:

> The modest Société founded by René Guilleré had grown and enriched itself; it had also officialized itself. In order to gain a place in the sun, the Décorateurs deemed it tactically advisable to place their leadership in the hands of politicians with an eye to the keys of the national palaces (I had almost written 'of Paradise') at their command. Committee members were prominent in ministries, and ministers were prominent at the Société's receptions and banquets.[14]

Their abstention at the Salon of 1929 and their announcement of the formation of the UAM was greeted with almost unanimous approval by the press. Most saw that without the young designers, the innovative element of the Société was lost, and they criticized Société artists for refusing to deviate from the luxurious formulas that they had established in 1925. Critic Louis Cherronet agreed that the Société no longer had a *raison d'être*, because their claim to support the creation of a modern style was no longer valid:

> In former times, the Société achieved its goal perfectly. It was a combative group. Why then this complacency towards money and commercial production, this search for easy and immediate praise, this taste for triumph without risk?[15]

Indeed, by 1929 the original goals of the Société seemed to have been virtually abandoned at the expense of seeking government recognition. Their insistence on seeing themselves as fine artists and their refusal to seek a real partnership with industry destroyed

157. Gabriel Englinger, Salon, 1928. Furniture in burr ash upholstered in mauve satin.

any possibility of providing good design to a large sector of the population. The problem indeed may have stemmed from the Société's practice since 1922 of soliciting aid from political figures who might defend their interests within the administration, instead of directing their efforts towards commerce and industry and the evolution of a modern style. Maurice Bokanowski, Société president since 1922, died in an air-plane crash in September 1928; he was

replaced by André Tardieu, Deputy from Belfort. Since Tardieu was busy with official functions, however, it was Charles Hairon, Société vice-president who assumed its day-to-day business. It is doubtful that Hairon, a wood sculptor who created decorative motifs for furniture and architectural details and a member of the association since 1910, greeted with enthusiasm the functionalist aesthetics proposed by Perriand, Herbst, Djo-Bourgeois and their colleagues. His position on this is indicated in his address to the Société in the spring of 1929:

Literary and artistic exchange between countries creates new needs, which industry wants to and can satisfy. While certain countries, and not among the least important, solicit the favour of the priority and exclusivity of our designs, others shamelessly plagiarize us. There are others which, all the while pro-

160. Edouard Bénédictus, Les Fruits d'or, 1925 (1927 Salon). Satin. Designed for Brunet-Meunié. Paris, musée des Arts décoratifs.

Left:

158. Léon Jallot, Dressing Table and stool, 1928 Salon. Sycamore, ivory and shagreen. Paris, galerie Arc-en-Seine.

159. Léon Jallot, Boudoir, 1928.

161. *Eugène Printz*, Interior for
a bibliophile and stamp collector.
Palmwood and metal,
vases by Jean Dunand.

claiming clearly defined economic frontiers related to their historical origins and ancestral culture, want to impose an international style on us. Such a supremacy would be fatal to nations and to artists whose art has not preserved the imprint of a fine race and a strong personality.[16] Through a change in its statutes, the Société definitively widened its separation from industry. Beginning in 1929, "The Salon is open to all creators, whether members of the Société or not, on the condition, however, that they do not also participate in exhibi-

tions reserved for industrialists."[17] In 1930, moreover, it announced that from that moment on, the Société would no longer participate in the industrial sections of international exhibitions, but only in the section reserved for the fine arts.[18]

Without the designers who left to found the Union des artistes modernes, the 1929 Salon was decidedly luxurious. The use of tubular steel decreased sharply from that of the Salon of the previous year. The majority of the furnishings still relied on fine craftsmanship and expensive materials: the

162. *Gilbert Poillerat, Door, 1928. Forged iron.*

163. *Michel Roux-Spitz, Bathroom, 1928. Dressing table and chair in sycamore, screen in aluminium and copper repoussé by Raymond Subes, floor in mosaïque and pâte de verre, lighting by Jean Perzel.*

Boudoir by Léon and Maurice Jallot, for example, was lacquered in gold and decorated with Cubist motifs. A cabinet designed by Henri Rapin displayed a complicated, hand-carved floral motif by Charles Hairon, in the style of the 1925 Exhibition. Apparently, only one year after its appearance at the Salon, a reaction against the brief flirtation with functionalism was already setting in. Yvanhoé Rambosson, one of the few critics who had something positive to say about the overall aspect of the exhibition, welcomed this return to sculpted wood furniture, an ancient French craft that he feared would be lost if it were not practised more often. Rambosson said that the move towards simplicity, straight lines and smooth, undecorated surfaces was far too easy for designers in other countries to copy, and would make French decorative arts lose their specific character: "Let us therefore combat this superstition held by some, according to which being modern consists of the exclusive cult of the straight line."[19] Rambosson's remarks suggest the disquieting position that both the Société and the State assumed vis-a-vis the avant-garde in design. The rejection of the "modernists" and the support of the *artisanat* would even be sanctioned by the administration. In December 1929, André François-Poncet, who had inaugurated the 1929 Salon as Under-Secretary of State for the Fine Arts, called for the establishment of a *politique des arts décoratifs*. In a chilling passage certainly coloured by the stock market crash of October 1929, he made it clear that the use of tubular steel and design for machine production would force artisans into unemployment:

> Let us repulse this rationalism that verges on unreason! French art, which has always lived of the free invention of its designers and the prodigious skill of its craftsmen, has nothing to gain by the success of geometric abstractions, international concepts, or the development of a 'standard' style that eliminates technical difficulties without resolving them, leaving our finest faculties unused, and condemning a large number of our artisans to unem-

ployment. . . . Let us remain attached to our national qualities, to tradition, to the virtues which until now have constituted our security! Let us flee from useless ornamentation and super—fluous niceties, but let us reject this sorry aridity that an immoderate dogmatism wishes to impose upon us. Midway between severity and a quasi-Oriental softness, let us guard this spirit of moderation that Paris has inherited from Athens, the guarantee of our present superiority and of our future triumphs![20]

As we shall see, this reaffirmation of craftsmanship would find support when the effects of the economic crisis began to be felt, and after the Société's confrontation with the functionalist designers of the Deutscher Werkbund at the Salon of 1930.

Suzanne Tise

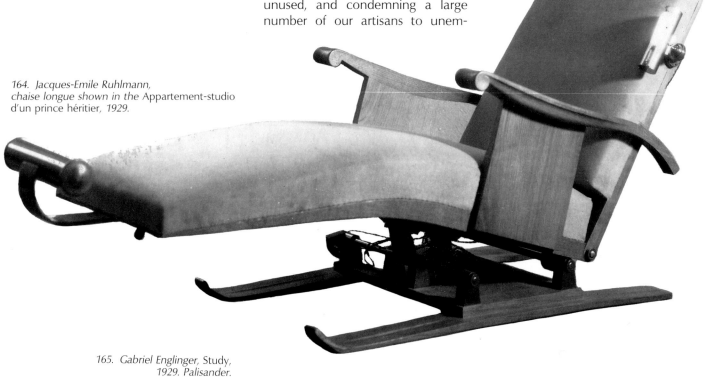

164. Jacques-Emile Ruhlmann, chaise longue shown in the Appartement-studio d'un prince héritier, *1929.*

165. Gabriel Englinger, Study, 1929. Palisander.

166. *Pierre Legrain, Bookbinding for*
La Canne de jaspe by Henri de Régnier.

11 May-8 July, Grand Palais

Organization of Salon:
Pierre Selmersheim, Michel Roux-Spitz,
Pierre Patout, Gauthier-Joseph Marrast,
Adolphe Dervaux
President: Maurice Bokanowski
Vice-presidents: Charles Hairon,
Henri Rapin, Maurice Dufrène
General Secretary: Geo Lamothe
Secretaries: Raymond Subes,
Raoul Lachenal
Treasurer: René Kieffer

The collective presentation of the French
Embassy at the Exposition des arts
décoratifs was an enormous success: the
battle against the copying of historical
styles had been won, and one of the main
goals of the Société, which was to asso-
ciate the modern decorative arts
movement with the Société in the eyes of
the administration and the public, had
been accomplished. Thirty-five members

received the Légion d'Honneur for their
contributions to the exhibition, among
them, those considered the most artistically "advanced" by their contemporaries:
Pierre Chareau and Mallet-Stevens.[21] At
the banquet offered in their honour at the
Hotel Lutetia, Pierre Rameil, Under-
secretary of Fine Arts, praised the renaissance in the decorative arts that had
resulted from the efforts of the Société, and
underlined the importance of its work to
France's prestige and to the national economy:

> You have been called upon to play a
> *capital role*, and believe me, I weigh my
> words, a capital role not only *in the
> artistic life, but also in the economic life
> of today and tomorrow*. We can count
> on you! Without vain chauvinism, I
> declare that in my eyes *French decor-
> ative arts* are the finest, the most 'chic'
> in the world, and I have no fear of being
> contradicted.[22]

In his introduction to the Salon catalogue,
Fernand David, Chief Commissioner of the
1925 Exhibition, exaggerated when he
claimed that the 1926 Salon demonstrated
a new concern with the needs of the
"average French person", but the collaboration between artists and manufacturers
was stronger here than ever before—more
than 60 artists were listed in the catalogue
as having worked with manufacturers.[23]
The workshops of the Printemps and
Galeries Lafayette department stores presented decorative schemes for entire
apartments. But the magnificent *Study for
an Art Collector* designed by Jacques-Emile
Rulhmann and the architect Alfred
Porteneuve remained the centrepiece of
the Salon. This room of monumental proportions was dominated by a grandiose
decorative painting by Alfred Janniot that
represented a stylized mythological scene,
and was furnished with the now-classic
Confort armchairs and canape designed by
Ruhlmann. This style of the *Bedroom*
by the young architect Georges Djo-
Bourgeois showed a preference for functionalism, marking an aesthetic division
among the members of the Société that
was to widen during the following years.
His interior was intended for the Villa that
Robert Mallet-Stevens was building for the
Viscount de Noailles in Hyères. Influenced
by the De Stijl movement, Djo-Bourgeois
took an original approach to interior design
by employing only built-in, geometric furnishings. The walls and the floor were
decorated with coloured squares and rectangles.

167. Paul Follot, Dining-room, designed for La Pomone.

168. Charlotte Perriand, Salon. Amboyna and palisander.

1926

170. *Jean Dunand,* Portrait of Madame Agnès.
Polychrome lacquer, eggshell.
Paris, private collection.

169. *Jacques-Emile Ruhlmann,*
in collaboration with Alfred Porteneuve,
Study for an Art Collector.
Left: Portrait of Madame Agnès
by Jean Dunand, decorative painting
by Alfred Janniot, sculptures
by Jean Bernard and François Pompon.

uly, Grand Palais

Yvonne Fourgeaud

aurice Bokanowski
nt: Charles Hairon
retary: Geo Lamothe
ené Kieffer

e Société embarked upon a
of applying modern art to
es through a special section of
evoted to the *Arts of the Street*
osters, publicity and designs for
f boutique façades and display
emonstrations of the ways that
hitecture and decoration could
draw attention to merchandise.
ion René Herbst designed a hall
op windows, some of which
pecial mannekins that he and
Lucie Holt Le Son created for
Siègel. The Société also held a
s of evenings of modern music,
nce, and fashion shows to
w their work fit into every
odern life.
ce of Cubism and a decorative
yle could be seen throughout
such as in the display of glass
ottles by Gaëtan Jeannin, and
sual geometric forms of the
especially in the ensembles by
lmann, Louis Sognot and Léon
this explosion of decorative
vas met with a certain
ss by critics like Leon Werth, a

175. René Buthaud, Vases.
Enamelled stoneware.

171. Jean Beaumont, Poster.
Paris, musée de la Publicité.

172. Etienne Kohlmann, Boudoir.
Designed for Studium Louvre.

173. Djo-Bourgeois, Dining-room.
*Table and chairs in folded aluminium,
fabric designs by Elise George.*

174. Jacques and Jean Adnet,
Studio/Smoking-room. *Peroba.*

176. Lucie Holt Le Son, Mannekin, Designed for the Maison Siégel. Sculpted wood.

177. Gaëtan Jeannin, Vases and Bowls.

supporter of the modern movement in furnishings since 1910, who asked just how "modern" the new Cubist style really was, and whether designers had not abandoned one worn-out decorative style—Art Nouveau—only to replace it with one that was equally superficial:

After the 1925 Exhibition of Decorative Arts, it is no longer possible to doubt the decline of ornamentation borrowed from the plant and animal kingdoms, or more generally—as the Germans say —naturalistic ornamentation. Modelled or stylized, the flower has been replaced by the triangle. Surfaces are being covered with regular or staggered, symmetrical or asymmetrical, juxtaposed, imbricated or overhanging geometric figures. In a word, ornamentation has become Cubistic. Whatever one may think of pictorial Cubism, it is a fact that the influence of Cubism can be found throughout the entire domain of ornament, and not only in furnishings. It inspires the posters in the street and one even sees women's shoes embroidered with Cubist motifs. But where furniture is concerned, it seems that we attribute to Cubist decoration a rigour that we deny to floral ornamentation. Perhaps there is a certain naïvety in this. An unnecessary triangle is no less an ornament than a superfluous rose, but for some reason, a designer can imagine that inherent in the representation of a triangle or a sphere, there is something of the rigour of a geometrical demonstration. . . .

The first duty was to fight against excessive ornament, garlands and scrollwork. Our modern eyes needed certitude and limpidity. Thus the designer found himself reduced to pure invention and restricted to an austerity of taste that could seem Calvinistic. No one doubts that the need to decorate, to modulate and break the monotony of surfaces is instinctual in primitive man, and that this tendency is degenerating in the instinct of civilized man. There were fears of packing-crate furniture and orthopaedic furniture, of baskets of roses and heaps of fruit. Cubist ornamentation was a compromise between the need for ornament and its satisfaction by means that now seem obsolete. Where the arbitrariness of a rose would have seemed intolerable, the arbitrariness of a triangle or of a sphere gave the illusion of rigour and necessity. Caprice disguised itself as geometry. The caprice of fashion itself.[24]

1928

178. *Charlotte Perriand, Djo-Bourgeois, and René Herbst joined to create a model apartment consisting of four rooms: a salon and kitchen by Djo-Bourgeois, a smoking-room by Herbst, and a dining-room by Perriand.*

179. *The* Dining-room *by Charlotte Perriand was furnished with a telescoping table* extensible, *and four* sièges tournants *covered in coral red leather. Although the interior was starkly simple and the surfaces textureless, Perriand achieved dramatic effects through a rich colour scheme—coral red and forest green—and through the association of natural and industrial materials.*

8 May-10 July, Grand Palais

Architecture: Pierre Montagnac, Henri Expert, Pierre Selmersheim, Henri Rapin, Joseph Hiriart, Georges Tribout, Georges Beau, Maurice Dufrène, Djo-Bourgeois

President: Maurice Bokanowski
Vice-presidents: Charles Hairon, Henri Rapin, Léon Bouchet
Treasurer: Henry Favier
Secretary General: Geo Lamothe
Secretaries: Maurice Daurat, Djo-Bourgeois

The 1928 Salon was a showcase for tubular steel furnishings, certainly influenced by the Die Wohnung exhibition held in Stuttgart the previous year that had been widely covered by the French art press. Critical response to the use of so much tubular steel at the Salon was ambivalent.

Société member Paul Brandt, writing in *Art et Industrie*, complained of the poor design of the models exhibited compared with those produced in Germany, and of the French designers' apparent ignorance of the material's structural possibilities.[25] Exception was made unanimously, however, for the interiors by Djo-Bourgeois, René Herbst and Charlotte Perriand. A critic writing for the *Journal d'Ameublement* praised their mastery of the aesthetic and structural potentials of tubular steel. Their group, he added, "sets the tone for the rest of the Salon. The public understands that these designers have adapted themselves to the demands of contemporary life, that they refuse to try to create an artificial style, and that they disregard the appearance of things and concern themselves with the study of the practical function of interiors."[26]

Aside from their group exhibit, several ensembles employing tubular steel furnishings were displayed by the department stores. For La Maîtrise of Galeries Lafayette, Maurice Dufrène created an interior for a country house that combined the innovative free-planning concepts of International Style architecture with an eclectic mixture of tubular steel and traditional wood furnishings. It consisted of a two-storey open space with a second-floor gallery overlooking the living-room. The various functional areas of the home (living-room, office, bedrooms, etc.), flowed freely into one another, but could be closed off by curtains hung on tubular steel rods. The furnishings were simple, but highly eclectic, including lounge chairs in tubular steel with comfortable curving upholstered cushions. Dufrène tried to make his essays in modern materials more palatable to a middle-class audience by juxtaposing them with more traditional models in wood, as in the wooden dining-room chairs upholstered in black patent leather.

180. In his Salon, Djo-Bourgeois created a powerful sculptural composition by the projecting balcony on the second level and the diagonal thrust of the staircase that descended into the room forming the framework of the divan. The two stools in tubular steel were elegant, but did not display the technological sophistication of contemporary German models.

181. René Herbst's Smoking-room was furnished entirely in tubular and sheet steel. The lounge chair was constructed of two continuous, curving steel tubes with a wide band of fabric forming the seat that seemed to be only draped over the frame.

182. In Maurice Matet's Woman's Study designed for Le Studium of the Grands Magasins du Louvre, the use of tubular steel was more an adherance to fashion than a genuine preoccupation with the economic and structural potentials of the material. As if to circumvent accusations that tubular steel was cold and unsympathetic, Matet's designs were deliberately decorative—he curved all the structural elements, and covered the chairs with heavily-tufted pigskin cushions. Throughout the interior he contrasted textures and materials for their decorative effect, as in the elegant asymmetrical desk in wood with tubular steel legs on one end.

1929

7 May-7 July 1929, Grand Palais

Architecture: Djo-Bourgeois,
Albert Laprade, Pierre Selmersheim
Organization of Salon:
Jacques-Emile Ruhlmann,
Alfred Porteneuve,
Marcel Chappey

President: André Tardieu
Vice-presidents: Charles Hairon,
Léon Bouchet, Henri Rapin
General Secretary: Geo Lamothe
Secretaries: Maurice Dufrène,
Pierre Montagnac
Treasurer: Henri Favier

183. René Gabriel, Catalogue cover, 1929.

184. Lucien Rollin, Study. *The rich tonalities of the furniture in ash and Swedish birch were juxtaposed with gleaming tubular steel.*

185. The Appartement-studio d'un prince-héritier *by Jacques-Emile Ruhlmann and Alfred Porteneuve was one of the most spectacular ensembles at the Salon. The desk in palisander was equipped with an electrically-heated footrest.*

Following double page:

186. Jules-Emile Leleu, Rotonde aménagée en salon dans une salle à manger. *Burl walnut.*

187. Jean Luce, Porto service and ashtrays. *Engraved crystal.*

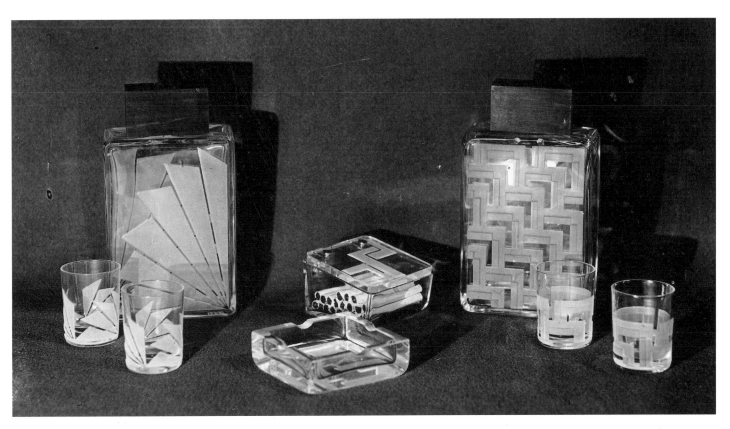

1930

The year 1930 was symbolic in the history of the Société des artistes décorateurs. After the more active and politically involved members left the association to form the Union des artistes modernes, the Société made room in its Salon for the participation of its first foreign group: the decorators, artists and craftsmen of the Deutscher Werkbund. The architect of the exhibition was Walter Gropius, the founder of the Bauhaus, assisted by his first collaborators from Weimar, Marcel Breuer, Herbert Bayer, and Moholy-Nagy. It was not surprising that their presence at the very heart of the Salon created an ambiguous situation that soon grew into a confrontation between two cultures.

The critics felt justified in expressing concern at a display of values that were completely opposed to those of French culture. These new values of the International Style, based on functionalism, were those to which Le Corbusier had been subscribing for more than a decade. They were also those upheld by the UAM, which opened the doors of its first salon at the Pavilion de Marsan almost simultaneously, in June 1930. A comparison of the two salons was inevitable, and it highlighted the differences within the UAM itself, particularly next to the exemplary unity of the Germans.

Although they gathered in 1929 in a sympathy of aesthetics and spirit around a steering committee composed of Hélène Henry, textile designer, Francis Jourdain, painter and furniture designer, René Herbst, interior architect, and Robert Mallet-Stevens, not all the founders of the Union des artistes modernes belonged to the international avant-garde movement. The UAM included artists who worked with Mallet-Stevens: master glassmaker Louis Barillet and sculptors Jean Prouvé and the Martel brothers. There were also the artists who had worked for Jacques Doucet: the sculptors Gustave Miklos and Joseph Csaky, the painter Etienne Cournault, who also worked with glass, and especially Pierre Legrain, who designed the UAM's logo before his death in July 1929. The group's first Salon presented a retrospective of Legrain's work that set the tone for the exhibition as a whole. While the Deutscher Werkbund at the Grand Palais displayed a family boarding house, a collective exhibit whose aestheticism was based on logic and economic realities, the UAM continued the practice of individual displays. Pierre Chareau expressed reservations about this in 1931 during a committee meeting, and asked for the abolition of stands in favour of a collective presentation, which corresponded more to his conception of what the UAM should be: a forum for ideas, not an interest group.

Luxury craftsmen, goldsmiths, jewellers and bookbinders also belonged to the UAM, as did Charlotte Perriand, a young decorator who started working in Le Corbusier's agency in 1927. There she devoted herself to an entirely new kind of furnishing programme, which she

189. *Walter Gropius,* Commons room for a Boarding House, *presented by the Deutscher Werkbund at the Salon of the Société des artistes décorateurs, 1930.*

Preceding page:

188. *Jean Dunand,* Boudoir, *Beige engraved lacquer. Salon of the Société des artistes décorateurs, 1930.*

presented for the first time at the Salon d'Automne of 1929. Her furnishings were later produced by Thonet. Perriand's *Equipement d'habitation* was a world of steel and glass: metallic furniture that worked in combinations to form partial or complete sets, seats of steel tubes and cloth stretched on springs, steel-tube tables and sheets of glass.[1] Part of this programme was exhibited at the Salon of the UAM in 1930. This constituted a complete break with the ornamental spirit of the designers of the Société and of the more widespread mode of crafts production.

When they came together to found an association in 1901, the members of the Société wanted to fight against the excesses and internationalism of Art Nouveau, setting their sights on a *Nouveau Style* nourished by French tradition. The UAM took up the same struggle and forged a militant, optimistic doctrine: the modern world against tradition, mass production against the luxury industries. Since it pursued the ideal of a synthesis of all the arts, it was open to artists from every discipline, but this soon gave the group an uncertain identity and diffused its original goals.

The UAM's Manifesto of 1934, intended as a response to virulent attacks in the reactionary press, stated positions which, more often than not, never went beyond wishful thinking: the social project elaborated by Le Corbusier, Charlotte Perriand and André Lurçat never got off the ground. In any case, and whatever their political opinions may have been, the jewellers of the UAM were obliged to work with the intellectual and financial elite.

Their relationship with industry continued to be a problem for the UAM, and the economic crisis reinforced a reactionary trend that had begun in 1931. The Société benefitted from this state of affairs at the expense of the dissidents, while the UAM continued to espouse a system of values that would not be put into practice until after the Second World War.

Yet, in 1930, everything was still possible. The position of the UAM was that of intellectuals who reject the established order. In 1932, some members joined the Association des écrivains et artistes révolutionnaires, which included such eminent figures in French literature as André Gide, André Malraux, Jean Guéhenno, and Paul Nizan.

Yvonne Brunhammer

190. View of the first Salon of the Union des artistes modernes, *1930.*
Sculpture by Jan and Joël Martel
and Gustave Miklos,
furniture by Jean Prouvé.

191. *Walter Gropius,* Gallery/Library
for a Boarding House,
furniture manufactured by Thonet.

In 1930, for the first time in its history, the Société des artistes décorateurs extended an invitation to a group of foreign artists to exhibit in its annual Salon. In July 1928, Docteur Grault, Director of the Grassi Museum in Leipzig and organizer of the 1927 Deutscher Werkbund exhibit there, sent an official request to the French Minister of Fine Arts asking if an exhibition of the German group could be held in Paris. The Société agreed to welcome the Werkbund to its spring Salon of 1930. This Salon immediately took on a significance that surpassed a typical exhibition of decorative arts: it would be the first time that German artists had been invited officially to exhibit in Paris since 1910. The exhibition would reveal not only radically different concepts of modern design, but also fundamental differences in national values.

The Deutscher Werkbund was founded in 1907 to raise German de-sign standards by encouraging co-operation between artists and industry. Under the leadership of pioneers of the modern movement such as Walter Gropius and Mies van der Rohe, it had become one of the most important cultural institutions in Germany, and by 1930, comprised nearly 3,000 architects, designers, craftsmen, university professors and industrialists.[1] Gropius, who had maintained close ties with the Werkbund since its foundation and who had resigned from the direction of the Bauhaus in 1928, was designated organizer of the Paris Exhibition. He chose former Bauhaus colleagues Marcel Breuer, Herbert Bayer, and Moholy-Nagy as his collaborators. The theme of the German exhibit was to design and furnish a ten-storey hotel/ boarding house. Gropius designed the plan for the steel-framed structure while Breuer and Bayer were respons-ible for the interior architecture and furnishings. Gropius outlined his intentions for the project to a French journalist a month before the exhibit: the show "would clearly demonstrate the new efforts towards rendering objective, on a technical and economic basis, all in art that until now had been personal and national". In Germany, he added, "these new tendencies are now accepted by the entire nation".[2] The exhibition "would draw attention especially to the standardized production of beautiful forms. This is not only the consequence of the rational point of view that dominates economic life today, but also a step along the way that leads to the cohesion of artistic endeavours and technical fabrication,

and that resolves the conflict between the spirit and reality."[3]

The Werkbund proposed an idealized model of collective living, incorporating the latest technical discoveries into domestic architecture. The scheme consisted of five rooms, including a model apartment designed by Breuer and separate displays of furnishings by Moholy-Nagy and Bayer. Gropius designed the communal spaces for the ensemble, featuring a coffee-bar and gallery/library with small "cells" underneath equipped for listening to music, playing cards, and reading. Also included were a gymnasium and pool. To divide the com-

192. Walter Gropius, Commons Room for a Boarding House.

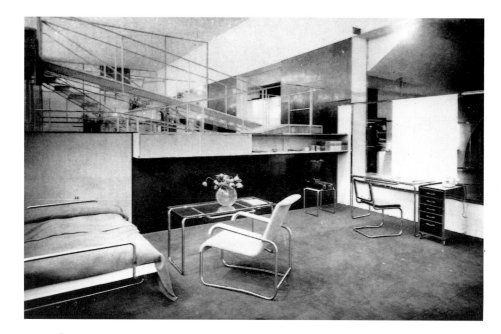

193. Marcel Breuer, Woman's Room
for a Boarding House.
Furniture manufactured by Thonet.

194. Marcel Breuer, Man's Room
for a Boarding House.
Furniture manufactured by Thonet.

munal area from the private apartments, Gropius constructed an ingenious steel bridge of standardized panels in grillwork that permitted visitors to view the installation from above.

Breuer's model apartment consisted of one room for a man, one room for a woman and an office adjacent to the man's room, sparsely equipped with his now well-known tubular steel furnishings mass-produced by Thonet. The two rooms converged on a small kitchen and bath. Breuer described his approach to the installation in the catalogue to the German section:

> There is one room per person for all purposes: living, reading, eating meals, sleeping, the bed serves as a lounge chair in the daytime. The man and the woman live independently and together: isolated and reunited by the antechamber, the bathroom and the kitchen.[4]

The man's room and the woman's room were virtually indistinguishable except for the addition of a globe and dark tones in the man's section, and a vase of flowers and a light colour-scheme in the woman's. Didactic texts were placed in each of the exhibition spaces explaining the function of the rooms and outlining the new style of life to be lived in them.

The displays by Moholy-Nagy and Bayer featured chairs in bent wood and tubular steel arranged in groups and suspended out from the walls, as well as various mass-produced objects like lamps and ceramics. Bayer also designed an innovative display of architectural photographs of previous Werkbund and Bauhaus projects that were hung from the walls and ceiling at angles intended to permit easier viewing by visitors. The catalogue in bold red and black print by Bayer was a masterpiece of typographical design. The part of the Salon organized by the Société had an entirely different theme: "A French Cultural Institute in a Foreign

195. Marcel Breuer, Apartment
for a Boarding House,
general view.

196. Herbert Bayer, Display
of photographs and architectural models.

197. Porcelain service, *Werkbund exhibit.*

198. *Edouard Bénédictus, Les Tulipes,
1925 (1930 Salon). Satin.
Designed for Brunet-Meunié.
Paris, musée des Arts décoratifs.*

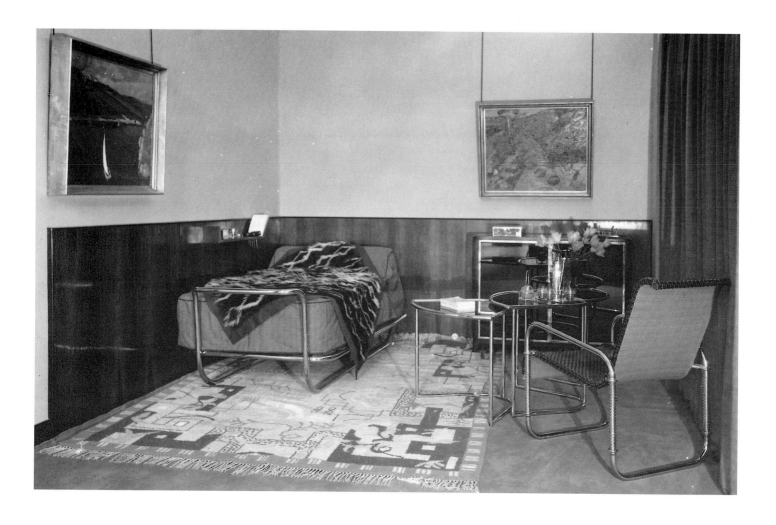

199. Etienne Kohlmann, Man's Bedroom. *Palisander, chromed metal and black glass.*

Country", devoted to the exhibition and diffusion of French art and luxury industries. The idea had arisen before the Werkbund accepted the invitation to the Salon, apparently in response to an announcement that the Ministry of Foreign Affairs was planning to purchase and furnish diplomatic *hôtels* in Prague, Luxemburg, Copenhagen and Santiago.[5] The progamme for the Salon, therefore, included designs for administrative services, an information office, a National Tourism Office, and apartments and reception rooms for ambassadors and attachés.

The section designed by the Société housed installations by nearly fifty individual designers. The general plan was laid out by architect R.H. Expert and Pierre Selmershiem, but each participant was responsible for the development and execution of his or her own stands, and this produced a wide range of styles and quality. The highly luxurious interiors of designers like Lalique and Ruhlmann featured beautifully-crafted wood furniture, one-of-a-kind pieces that continued the ancient French tradition of *ébénisterie*. But the Salon also included contemporary designs by Djo-Bourgeois and Etienne Kohlmann that relied on man-made materials such as chromed steel, glass and rubber. Even the most "modern" of the interiors, however, predominantly employed

*202. Jean Perzel, Lamp shown
in the Office for an Administrator
by Michel Roux-Spitz.*

*200. Jean Colosiez, Pierre Paschal
and Jean Merot du Barre,
Tourism Office.*

*201. Michel Roux-Spitz,
Office for an Administrator.*

1930

203. René Gabriel, Studio designed
for the art critic Léon Chanserel.
Sycamore and chromed model.

204. René Prou and Henri Martin,
Grand Salon de réception.

wood, contrasted occasionally with gleaming steel and glass details. The luxurious *Office for an Administrator* by Michel Roux-Spitz (intended for his own architectural firm) was typical of this approach to man-made materials. He carefully sculpted the interior space with an arrangement of built-in bookcases and a multi-functional L-shaped desk. The dark lacquered furniture was raised on brilliant steel bases, and the sleek, unmodulated surfaces and low, horizontal lines produced an effect of sober efficiency. For the *Studio* measuring 2 m 60 by 3 m 50 designed for writer and art critic Leon Chanserel,

René Gabriel took on the challenge of making the most of a restricted space. He installed both a working and a sleeping area, combining sycamore wood with glass and chromed steel. More traditional interiors were also displayed, such as René Prou's *Grand salon de réception.* Its furnishings were executed by La Pomone (Bon Marché). The *Chambre de dame* by Eugène Printz provided a perfect example of the suprising eclecticism that could result from a designer's confrontation with metal—the decorative frames of the bed and armchair were sheathed in tufted satin.

205. Eugène Printz, Woman's Bedroom.

One characteristic feature of the French section was the search for dramatic effect in the architectural design of both domestic interiors and public spaces through an interplay of large masses. Few of the interior's plans were simple squares or rectangles. The *Tourism Office* by Colisiez, Barré and Paschal was a sweeping, oval-shaped hall punctuated by a series of oval pilasters. A large cupola was dramatically illuminated from below by a suspended steel disk. A similar theatrical effect was sought by Pol Abraham and Henry Le Même in their *Exhibition Hall* with its juxtaposition of shimmering tile and steel and the sense of movement created by the concave walls and convex pillars.

In contrast to the negative press of the two previous salons, French critical reaction to the Société's presentation was on the whole very positive. Most felt that the arid and impersonal environments of the Werkbund easily demonstrated the superiority of the French approach of beauty and comfort. Despite high regard for the organizational and technical proficiency of the Werkbund, the efforts of the German designers were met with intense criticism that focused on several issues. For many French critics, it was not the Werkbund's almost exclusive use of steel that was so unacceptable, but its entire approach to art; it seemed antithetical in every way to French values and traditions.

One of the most elaborate and scathing critiques of the German section was made by Pierre Lavedan, in *L'Architecture*, the official review of the *Société des architectes diplômés par le gouvernment*. His article sums up the views of most of the critics who wrote about the 1930 Salon. According to Lavedan:

> The great interest of the German section is not so much that it offers new forms, but that it invites us to

206. Eugène Printz, Dressing Table *shown in* Woman's Bedroom.

207. Walter Gropius, Staircase and Bridge *constructed of standardized elements.*

208. Michel Dufet, Office, designed for
the Compagnie royale asturienne des mines.

209. Michel Dufet, Armchair, lacquered metal.
Designed for the Office of the Compagnie
royale asturienne des mines.

210. Michel Dufet, Desk (1947). Zinc.
The original model, designed in 1929 without
the red lacquer on the disks, was shown
first at the Salon d'Automne in 1929,
and then in the Office Dufet designed
for the Compagnie royale asturienne des mines
presented at the Salon of the Société
des artistes décorateurs in 1930.

reconsider certain values: artistic, moral and social. The Deutscher Werkbund proposes to substitute other values for those which have ruled all of art, and French art in particular; we might even say all of French society.[6]

For Lavedan the new principles proposed by the Werkbund were basically 1) the non-individuality of the artist, 2) the functionalism of art, and 3) the collectivism of art. In his opinion, art had traditionally been treated as a question of individual genius. The same artistic problem, then, could have many solutions. The Werkbund, however, suggested that the individual cachet an artist gave to a work could be eradicated entirely. In the German section it was impossible to tell the difference between one artist's work

211. *Eugène Printz, Two armchairs (contemporary upholstery). Paris, galerie l'Arc-en-Seine. Shown in the Salon (illustrated fig. 212).*

and another's, and, what is more, nothing had been included that did not respond to a strictly utilitarian purpose. From this Lavedan surmised that the Germans had replaced the inspiration of the artist with calculated scientific research.[7] This notion led Lavedan to the second principle of the Werkbund: the functionalism of art. He condemned it for two basic reasons. In the first place, the currently fashionable word "functionalist" was nothing new.

212. Eugène Printz, Salon.

After all, he declared, "The great classical French thinkers, and Descartes first of all, long ago stated the better part of these principles, but we generally forget this because they did not do so with any aggressiveness." Second, the Werkbund had carried functionalism too far by implying that art had no place in a modern society except to fulfill a purpose:

The old romantic cry of Cyrano: 'It is much more beautiful when is is

useless', is decidedly outmoded. There is hardly need to add that what will disappear first is whatever decorates.

On the last point, the collectivity of art, Lavedan was even more acerbic:

The Deutscher Werkbund, elevating itself to the rank of prophet, represents the human being of tomorrow as subject to strict rules of equality. Everything will have to be 'typified', or if you prefer another barbarism,

213. Jean Dunand, Vestibule *with decorative lacquered panel, "Eléphants".*

'standardized'. And I mean everything: not just furniture, but man also. Our successors . . . will lead the standard existence which many of us have known in the barracks.[8]

He ended by praising the humanism of the French approach, contrasting it to the Werkbund's self-effacing slavery to a single idea and its attempt to socialize artistic thought:

Our hesitation is due to our feeling for the complexity of human nature and to the refusal to sacrifice half of the universe to a theoretical affirmation of unity.[9]

This disapproval was echoed in some form or another by French critics in nearly all of the Salon reviews. For Marcel Zahar, writing in *Art et Industrie*, what the German section lacked was "charm". The furnishings, he said, "look too much like the detached parts of a machine, the rooms lack charm—this intangible thing which would have created a softer atmosphere of intimacy".[10] For Zahar, the essential difference between the French and German designers was this: while the Germans presented only a schematic and abstract vision of the domestic interior, the French carried their ideas to fully-realized conclusions, creating environments of atmosphere and intimacy. Gaston Varenne seconded this view, seizing upon the failure of the Werkbund to consider the aesthetic as well as the material needs of the human being:

> I insist on this point: the modern and French artist does not believe he has accomplished his task by ignoring aesthetic concerns or the desire to please.[11]

Apparently, then, what the French critics saw themselves defending in 1930 was not merely a question of artistic liberty: the survival of an entire culture was at stake. Gaston Varenne certainly believed this when he warned his readers of the moral and artistic bankruptcy of the anti-individualism proposed by the Werkbund designers, who renounced:

> All play of decorative forms to speak a new, abstract, international language. . . . The reign of individualism is finished, we are told. We have arrived at a stage of civilization where all that matters is the standardization of life. . . . And the citizen of our times is portrayed as demanding a rigid armature to firmly surround him, the only means for him to live intensely the life of the nation and to renounce his miserable and vain existence.[12]

Varenne went even further to explain that these ideas were not only found in Germany, but among the avant-garde of all countries. As a matter of fact, the real source of this wave of egalitarianism was not Germany, but the United States. The exhibition was in fact "the direct reflection of concepts which America is trying to impose on the world, a hidden threat to the principles

214. Jean Dunand, Vase. Lacquered gold metal. Musée d'Art moderne de la Ville de Paris.

215. *Etienne Kohlmann,* Woman's Bedroom.

on which our European culture has gradually been built". And he added emphatically,

> France owes it to itself to remain faithful to its tradition, to its long past of artistic glory and to maintain in art the superiority which has always been recognized in the finish of its production and in the quality of its craftsmen.[13]

It may be taken for granted that the German critics of the French section had equally negative observations to make about the Société's presentation. As Wilhelm Lotz remarked in his review of the Salon for the Werkbund magazine, *Die Form*, the Werkbund display was simply representative of the preoccupations of a new international movement. He contrasted the social consciousness of modern German design with the French adherence to high-quality craftsmanship:

> A great number of men in all the civilized countries, driven by the same ideas and possessing the same rights, stand behind this work. This will and this effort carry in themselves a great moral strength; that is to say, the possibility for all humanity to benefit from all modern productions.[14]

For Lotz, while tradition-bound France had closed its eyes to the pressing social and economic conditions of the modern world, preferring to cater to the whims of an elite, modern Germany had presented the true and moral solution to modern design. France made pretty objects, he said, but they really had no meaning in contemporary society:

> What is unquestionable is that if nothing was shown pertaining to the great intellectual, social and economic problems which we must attend to today, this exhibition would have had the character of a private fancy, and not that of a forum for vast and important ideas.[15]

Beyond these issues of art, style and culture, there was in the Salon of 1930 yet another dimension, one both political and economic. Not only did the Werkbund make a *tabula rasa* of tradition and insert an abstract, international language of forms in its place. The Werkbund asserted that it would establish the new norm for design, that German standards would be the international standards. This was an assertion that raised frightening questions about France's position on the European economic and political stage. One anonymous writer in an article entitled "Hypermodernisme" said this about the real meaning of the Werkbund display:

> The only truly modern nation, the one which understands clearly the conditions and needs of the future, has already purged its spirit of all the old-fashioned hotchpotch which is still called decorative art. This nation, of course, is Germany. A policy of intimidation, of massive affirmation whose commanding tone makes for authority.... There is thus a will, and economic policy at the origin of 'modern' aesthetic endeavours.[16]

It is difficult to say how the public reacted to the 1930 Salon, but the reaction of the French press to the Werkbund exhibit is important, because it helps to explain the violence of the attacks against modern design that developed during the early 1930s. At that time, hundreds of artisans and designers found themselves out of work during the devastating economic crisis that rocked Europe, and the whole premise of industrial culture was being called into question. These attacks, chauvinistic, of course, would merit to be forgotten if they were not at the base of a virulent anti-rationalism that would begin to reveal itself during the following year.

Suzanne Tise

216. Herbert Bayer, Presentation of chair models designed by Marcel Breuer, Luckhardt and Anker Brothers, and Adolf Schneck.

217. *René Gabriel, Catalogue cover.*

219. Gabriel Englinger, Dining-room. Walnut.

218. *Standardized utensils in porcelain.*

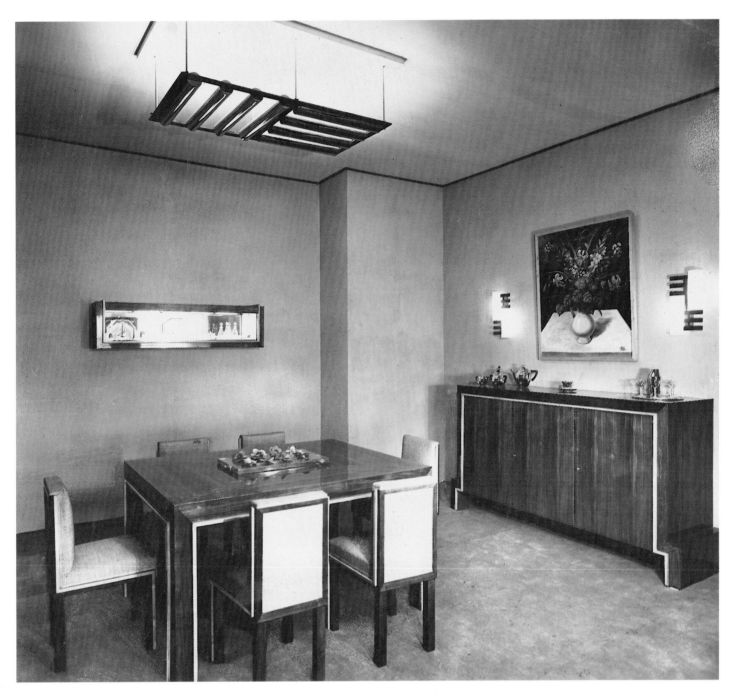

15 May-13 July, Grand Palais

President: André Tardieu
Vice-presidents: Charles Hairon,
Henri Rapin, Pierre Montagnac
General Secretary: Geo Lamothe
Secretaries: Lucie Renaudot, Paul Bablet
Treasurer: Raymond Subes

Architecture of the French Section:
Henri-Roger Expert, Pierre Selmersheim
Organization of Salon: Charles Siclis,
Jacques-Emile Ruhlmann,
Alfred Porteneuve, Henri Rapin,
Raymond Gravereaux, Maurice Daurat,
Denis Bablet, Raymond Subes, Léon Jallot

Committee of the German Section:
Ernst Jaeckh, Guenther von Pechmann,
Eric Raemisch

Architecture: Walter Gropius
Organization: Herbert Bayer,
Marcel Breuer, Moholy-Nagy

Excerpt from the introduction by Charles
Hairon to the catalogue of the French
section:
The importance of the German section
organized by the Werkbund attests to
the prestige attained by our group and
to the interest of an event that permits
the works of artists from different
schools to be shown under the same
roof.
Our visitors will thus be able to compare
the various solutions adopted for ident-
ical architecture and interior design
problems by artists from two neigh-
bouring countries whose realizations
symbolize the spirit and and intellectual

and social tendencies of their people.
The ensemble conceived by Professor
Walter Gropius will no doubt present a
different solution from that of the French
section. The leader of the German section, by treating a theme chosen especially by himself, imposed a discipline
on all of his collaborators—artists, manufacturers, merchants—whom he united
under his direction to serve a national
ideal. The subject proposed to its exhibitors by the Société des artistes
décorateurs, 'A French Cultural Institute
in a Foreign Country', was more theoretical than absolute, more of a pretext to
dissertation than a problem to solve. . . .
It is possible that this will emphasize the
independent character of our own colleagues even more. Our Society in-
cludes artists of all tendencies, all de-

181

sirous of asserting their individuality as much as possible.

Excerpt from the catalogue of the German section:

The section organized by the Deutscher Werkbund is representative of the German spirit of today. The Werkbund is comprised of avant-garde personalities from all domains of art. Its principle is that the use of choice materials is not enough to ensure quality. Quality can be obtained only through an exact idea of the practical use of each object so that the appropriate form can be found that corresponds to its function. This form must express both practical and spiritual meaning. . . .

The presentation of the Deutscher Werkbund at the invitation of the Société des artistes décorateurs français, should thus be considered as proof that there is a close relationship between all modes of artistic expression; in the fields of architecture, housing, theatre, objects of everyday life, and the social and industrial life in which we live. No object of everyday use can escape this rule.

The exhibition will therefore show pieces produced in series and through a scientific conception, which nonetheless show a concern for beauty. The exhibitors believe that they have reached a milestone in the alliance between aesthetics and technology.

1931-1942

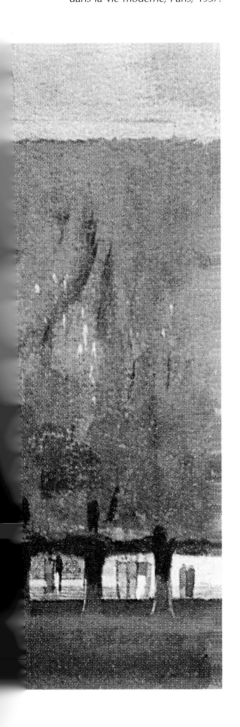

This decade, which shook Western values and ended in a major world conflict, was reflected in the attitude of the Société. The group rejected the uncertainties of French politics and veered more towards conservatism than reform. While the members of the UAM, or at least those who were the most politically involved, followed the actions of the Popular Front, the Société, under the presidency of André Tardieu, sank its roots deeper into national tradition.

The Société turned to the eternal values of Art and unified action to protect itself from the economic crisis that had lodged within the sector of artistic production. Shortsightedly, it championed a return to traditional techniques, materials and craftsmanship (later one of the main ideological thrusts of the Vichy government). The decorator André Arbus was among those who were in favour of the crafts tradition. For the Paris Exposition internationale des arts et techniques dans la vie moderne in 1937, he designed a *Residence in the Ile-de-France* contrasting a world charged with humanity and intimacy to the industrial inferno. The wood furniture possessed a simple, classical design.

The tension between the Société and the UAM reached its peak at the 1937 Exhibition. The exhibit claimed to reject the original theme of the decorative arts in favour of crafts and techniques applied to modern life, but in fact it followed the official line of rehabilitating the crafts, a movement that had begun six years earlier at the Colonial Exhibition of African and Asian arts.

The artistes décorateurs chose Pierre Patout, the architect of Jacques-Emile Ruhlmann's *Hôtel d'un collectionneur* at the 1925 Exhibition, to create the decor for an "eloquent . . . symbol, the most conclusive demonstration of the role and virtue of the decorative arts". The UAM, meanwhile, had its own pavilion by the Seine, despite the conflicts that had arisen between its representatives and the associations responsible for the programme. The Popular Front, elected to the head of the government in May 1936, supported the modern tendency. When Charlotte Perriand was asked by Minister Georges Monnet to build the Pavilion of Agriculture, she accepted, and used the display to illustrate the Popular Front's projects. Among the measures taken at the beginning of Socialist rule was the creation of an Under-Secretary of State for Sports and Leisure—which was criticized by the right as an incitement to idleness. This innovation was nonetheless a product of the spirit of the times. Sports and outdoor life, symbols of physical and moral health, were recognized as being the right of everyone. They demanded a specific decorative repertoire, as well as new concepts in housing, typified in displays at the Société's Salons, ranging from the *Home of a Sportsman* to a *Week-end House*. A young man's home or studio was the theme of major displays in 1935, both at the Société Salon by Suzanne Guiguichon,

224. Unemployed artists in Paris, c. 1935.

and at the Brussels Universal Exposition by UAM members Charlotte Perriand, Louis Sognot and René Herbst. In the Société Exhibit, sports were evoked through photographs; the UAM showed a physical exercise room, which Herbst treated as an open, functional space.

Sports, a pretext for some, a fundamental choice for others, was in any case a new element in French life between the two World Wars. It was a means of social mobility, serving as a bridge between the strata of society. It was one small certitude in a civilization that was questioning its very foundations.

Einstein's discoveries put an end to traditional theories of knowledge, and opened the way for the work of Joliot and Louis de Broglie. The 1937 Exhibition provided an opportunity to put science at the service of the public. The creation of the Centre national de recherche scientifique in 1936 and of the musée de l'Homme one year earlier was the work of the Popular Front, which considered the State responsible for both upholding and facilitating the spread of knowledge.

The 1930s were divided between the desire to raise the cultural level of the masses by increasing the flow of information and the terrifying rise of Fascism in Europe. Intellectuals, scientists, writers and artists

226. Surrealist decors in the Pavilion of Elegance, *architect: Etienne Kohlmann. Exposition internationale des arts et techniques dans la vie moderne, Paris, 1937.*

225. *Le Corbusier, Pierre Jeanneret, Charlotte Perriand,* La maison du jeune homme, *Universal Exposition, Brussels, 1935.*

became intensely political, while the concepts of Left and Right lost much of their meaning. Curiosity and invention were rife. The French bourgeoisie, the chief customer of the artistes décorateurs, was not open either to the questioning of scientific certitudes or the vision of the world such questions implied. It ensconced itself in a status quo of which the 1939 Société Salon was the surrealistic reflection. Combined with the Salon de la Lumière, it presented a *Street at night*, a street that belonged to the realm of fantasy, where the houses were not true houses. "We have not tried to be real", the introduction to the catalogue stated. Prepared in the midst of the menace and clatter of arms, this last Salon before the war claimed to defend spiritual values. The result was impressive, classical and theatrical—a world of false luxury and ornamentation exaggerated to the breaking point. While France slid towards the gloom of the war years, a World's Fair was inaugurated in New York in the summer of 1939. It afforded a look at a civilization that Europe would discover only five years later, one dominated by industry and the power of large corporations.

Yvonne Brunhammer

227. *Pierre Selmersheim, Exhibition hall, 1931 Salon. Decorative paintings by Henry Marret.*

228. *Eugène Printz, Cabinet, 1932. Palisander, marquetry in tortoise shell and metal. Paris, musée des Arts décoratifs.*

During the 1930s, the activities of the Société des artistes décorateurs were determined by the economic, social and political crises that struck the nation during the decade. More than at any other time in its history, the Salons became the reflection of an age: it is possible to read in the actions of the Société, and in the aesthetic decisions of its members, the sense of profound disarray that confronted the Parisian artistic community in these *années tournantes.*[1]

In 1930, eighteen additional members resigned from the Société, among them some of its most accomplished talents—Maurice Dufrène, Lucie Holt Le Son, Louis Sognot, Jean Prouvé, and Fernand Nathan.[2] Because of this, and the earlier departure of the artists who formed the Union des artistes modernes, the Salon of 1931 showed little of the variety that had characterized previous Salons. The change in the Salon's overall atmosphere was striking: the decorative exuberance that sprang from the 1925 Exhibition and the lively Cubist motifs that covered furnishings, walls and floors had entirely disappeared. Furnishings no longer possessed precise, geometric contours, and seemed heavier, even lugubrious, compared to those of the year before. A pronounced

move towards neo-classicism could be seen in the architecture of the halls and exhibition galleries, and it was even more obvious in the special section reserved for figurative sculpture and a retrospective exhibit devoted to the sculptor Joseph Bernard.

The main preoccupation of the Société was to find ways to shield its members from the effects of the economic crisis that were beginning to make themselves felt in numerous areas of artistic production in France. Successive cur-

rency devaluations in the three other largest industrialized nations—Great Britain, Germany, and the United States—had begun to paralyse exports, and the luxury goods industries were among the hardest hit. In November 1931, the Société published a call for unity among its membership, insisting that only the maintenance of their faith in high artistic ideals could protect them where their faith in progress had failed:

Against the blind forces of economic

229. *Henri Favier,* Rotunda Jean Goujon, *1931 Salon. Exhibition of sculpture by Joseph Bernard.*

laws, isolated men are disarmed, but they can struggle and resist if they form a bloc of their common aspirations and rights, and thus give their professional value a social importance. Our professional worth at this time is capital for France, for we are as necessary to Art as scientists in their laboratories are to industry. At a time when financial powers tend to suffocate all ideals, more than ever we must loudly proclaim that a civilization without art is a body without a soul; and we must prove by our actions and our work, that if money permits realization, it is only the spirit that creates.[3]

Recourse to the eternal values of art in the face of economic calamity would seem natural and even admirable had it not provided the foundations for a widespread and pernicious anti-modernist campaign supported by a substantial sector of the building and decoration industries. We have seen how the French press reacted to the high technology of the Werkbund designers in 1930; these same critiques would be leveled against French designers who worked in a similar mode.[4] The situation exploded with the publication of a series of pamphlets and articles by the designer Paul Iribe (1883-1935), well known since the 1910s for his work for the couturiers Paul Poiret and Jacques Doucet. In 1931, for example, he published an article entitled "Profits and Losses" in the trade journal *Ameublement et Décoration* in which he denounced the ruinous effects of the machine not only on the French arts industries but also on Western civilization:

> The blind triumph of the machine ends in a tragic disaster for all of Humanity. . . . Under the threat of famine or revolt, we must return to the HAND the tools which it has abandoned and which it no longer knows how to use. Men between the

230. Mathurin Méheut, Ceramic tiles, *1933.*

231. *Jean Dunand, Vase, 1932.*
Lacquered metal.
Paris, galerie Couvrat-Desvergnes.

232. *Jacques-Emile Ruhlmann*
and Alfred Porteneuve, Un Rendez-vous
de pêcheurs de truites, 1932.

ages of eighteen and thirty will have
to learn, to understand, and to LOVE
a manual skill, learn to use a tool:
pick, hammer, plane, pencil. . . . We
must decide this very day what will
follow. The problem may be stated
in two words: 'Standardization or
Individuality'.[5]

He continued his campaign in February
1932, in a speech he gave before a
gathering of the *Corporations du
bâtiment*, denouncing the ruinous effects on French decoration of ideas
from Germany and Switzerland (here
he meant the Werkbund and Le
Corbusier). His speech was later published in a beautifully-designed pamph-
let entitled *Défense du luxe*:

We have renounced French stone
for cement. We have renounced
French architecture for German
architecture. We have renounced
French furniture for the cube, and
French wood for plywood. . . . This
crime of *lèse-patrie* was accentuated
by the costliest commercial mistake
that we could have made; we forgot
the axiomatic truth that a French
product sells in the world because it
is French, but that an 'interna-
tionalized' product can be sold in
the world only on the basis of commercial and industrial competition, a
concept which has always escaped
us. We have abandoned the
exclusivity of our exceptional products, and accepted the competition
of prices![6]

Iribe's statements were commented
upon widely in the French press, which
in general seconded his view that
France's faith in industrial progress had
destabilized the foundations of the
national economy, and praised his
recommendation that a return to
traditional French *métiers* would protect artists and artisans from the effects
of the economic crisis.[7] Similar opinions
were put forward by the architect
Gustave Umbdenstock in a conference
in the Salle Wagram in 1932, where he
invited members of the decoration and
building trades stricken by unemployment to testify before the audience of the disastrous effects of "international cement" and "ultra-rationalist"
architectural formulas.[8]

That the return to French traditions,
materials, and techniques had become
a question of patriotism and national
interest could be seen at the Société's
Salon in 1932, where tubular steel was
abandoned for solid woods orna-
mented with decorative bronzework.
Jacques-Emile Ruhlmann's *Rendez-
vous des pêcheurs* could not have
been more symbolic of the rejection of
urban, industrial civilization. At the
1933 Salon, this tendency was even
more marked; designers sought the

revival and participation of some of the most traditional French industries for elements like tapestry work or decorative, engraved glass. There was also new interest in mural painting—but now celebrating the virtues of the land, as in Lotiron's *Moissoneurs*. Ceramics and metal work demonstrated a deliberate lack of sophistication in their profiles and decoration, as in the work presented by Mayodon, Meheut and Du Mont. The idea, however, was not to return to primitive methods of craft production, but to reestablish a more immediate contact between the artisan and his or her materials and techniques (a contact believed to have been lost with the advent of mechanization), and at the same time adapt design to more contemporary needs and methods of production. This is how the designer André Arbus explained the "return to tradition" in an article entitled "Furniture and Individual Needs", published in the *Encyclopédie française*:

A new current of thought, tired of submission to the machine, is trying to encourage a renaissance of manual work and a revival of regional traditions. It is certain that the sight of handmade objects is an appealing one for man. The return to ancient formulas and techniques, solid

235. Alfred Lombard, Decorative painting
shown in the Salle des fêtes
designed by Pierre Selmersheim, 1933.

Left page:

233. Robert Lotiron, Les Moissonneurs, 1932.

234. Georges Serré, Vase, 1933. Stoneware.

236. Pierre du Mont, Vases, 1933.
Hammered pewter.

237. Pierre Bobot, The Races in Auteuil,
1933. Two-panel lacquered screen.

239. André Arbus, Woman's Desk and Chair,
1932. Ebony and grey satin.

238. Jacques-Emile Ruhlmann, Woman's desk,
1933. Violet wood, ebony, leather, lizard skin.
Paris, musée des Arts décoratifs.

1931-1942

*240. Jean Luce, Tea Service, 1933, Faïence.
Paris, galerie Couvrat-Desvergnes.*

242. Maurice Dufrène, Dining-room, 1935. Oak.

Left page:

241. Lucien Rollin, Dining-room, 1935.

243. René Gabriel, Equipment for a dining-room and for a bedroom in juxtaposable elements, 1935.

244. *Eugène Printz, Cabinet, 1933.*
Palisander and metal.
Musée d'Art moderne de la Ville de Paris.

wood, for example, which bring decoration back with them as if by vital necessity, must permit the worker to add the living grace of personal execution to the abstract beauty of pure proportions. . . . This new orientation of ideas is proof of . . . the desire to liberate the decorative arts from the paralysing quest for novelty. Returning to the source, to principles, it attests to a will to give to the furniture-maker his last chance, and challenges the peril of extinction which threatens him.[9]

This new attention to individual human needs, the return to more "humanist" values, tradition, and *métier* reached its apogy at the Salon of 1935 in designs dubbed by the press "modernized tradition"and "rustic modern". Decorators tried to find a compromise between the *nudisme intégral* of the

245. *Eugène Printz, Table, 1934.*
Paris, galerie Dutko.

machine style, and the need for a rational organization of the interior that could also incorporate indigenous woods, natural materials, and a wide variety of crafts. This was clearly the approach taken by Maurice Dufrène in his oak *Dining-room*, in which the smooth surfaces and straight lines were given a "hand-made" look by decorative additions of brass tacks and leather. Work by regional craftsmen

Following double page:

*247. André Lagrange, Smoking-room
of the Oceanliner Normandie,
lacquered panels by Jean Dunand,
1935. Watercolour.*

*246. Suzanne Guiguichon, Studio, 1935.
Oak, hand-woven linen.*

was also presented, as in the rustic ensemble of the *ébénistes* from Dinan. Some of the most successful applications of this trend could be found in interiors by René Gabriel and Suzanne Guiguichon that demonstrated a rational arrangement of space, an emphasis on elegance and comfort, and a use of a variety of natural materials such as blond woods, thick wools and cottons, and floor coverings in blond quartzite or terra cotta.

Two important national projects intended to breathe new life into the flagging decoration industries were conceived during the 1930s. The project for the luxury ocean-liner

Normandie, announced by the Compagnie générale transatlantique in 1931, provided work for hundreds of artists and craftsmen, many of whom were members of the Société. But it was in the project for the "Exposition internationale des arts et techniques dans la vie moderne", scheduled for 1937, that the various *corps de métiers* and the Société placed their highest hopes for a solution to the serious unemployment problem.

The first project for the exhibition, however, was developed before the crisis reached France. It was proposed at the National Assembly in November 1929 as an exhibition of modern decor-ative and industrial arts similar to the one in 1925. The project was officially adopted in June 1930.[10] Afterwards, however, the programme underwent several transformations, direct results of the social and economic crisis—the proposition in the Senate in 1932 for an Exposition de coopération intel-lectuelle, and the idea of the Paris City Council of an exhibition devoted to "worker and peasant life". Mounting pressure from the various interest groups involved led the government to decide upon an exhibition that incor-porated all three proposals into an enormous international manifestation scheduled for 1937.[11]

250. Grand Salon of the oceanliner Normandie, 1935. Decorative panels by Jean Dupas, pewter vase by Maurice Daurat, furniture by Jean M. Rothschild.

248. Jean Dunand, La Chasse, panel forming part of the decorative cycle in the smoking-room of the oceanliner Normandie, 1935. Incised gold lacquer.

249. Pierre Patout and Henri Pacon, Departure Hall of the oceanliner Normandie, 1935.

251. Max Vibert, Poster.
Paris, musée de la Publicité.

252. Michel Dufet, Child's Bedroom, 1936.
Wallpaper design by Denise Louvet.

As the various projects were being debated, the Société tried to win for itself the artistically central place that it had occupied in the 1925 exhibition through a major architectural and decoration project. The committee held a series of unofficial meetings with the Ministry of Fine Arts in the spring of 1931, but without being able to obtain any real assurances, as it later reported to the Société's General Assembly:

We are against no one, we accept all collaborations, we would collaborate on all projects which preserve the interests of our Société and the in-tegrity of our comrades, but it should be understood that . . . we shall demand our place, a place at least as large as in 1925. If we do not obtain it, we will be disciplined enough to stage a strike which could prevent any manifestation at all from taking place.[12]

In December 1931, the Société assembled a permanent committee, together with the Société des architectes modernes, the Union des artistes modernes, the Société des artistes français, and the Société nationale des beaux-arts, to coordinate efforts, pre-

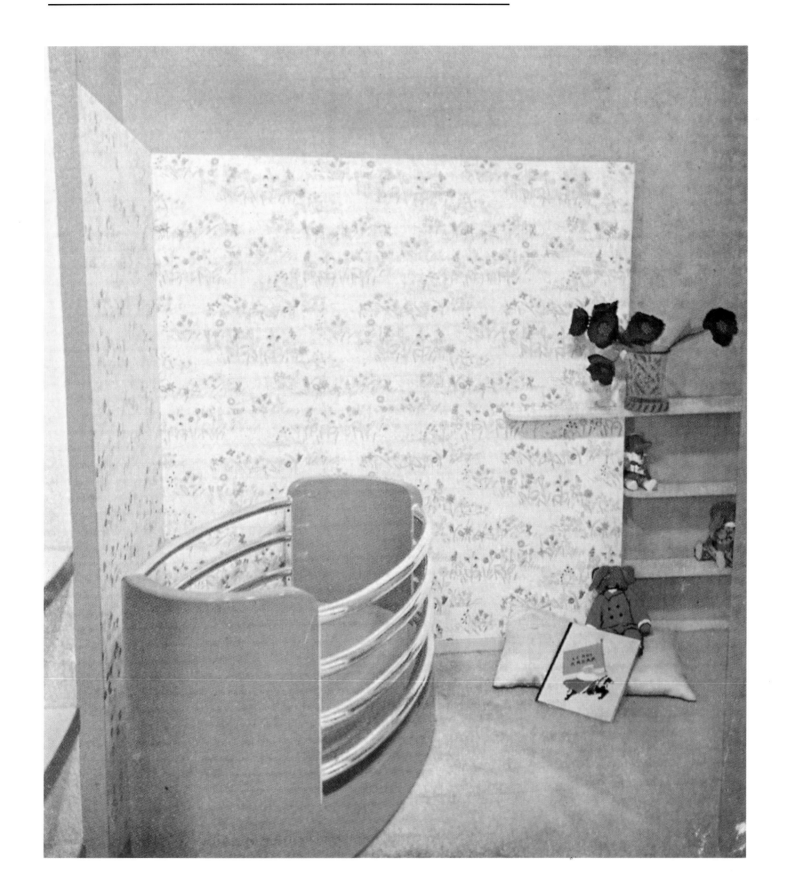

253. Interior of the Pavilion of the Union des artistes modernes, *Exposition des arts et techniques dans la vie moderne, 1937. Architect Georges-Henri Pingusson, Mural painting by Fernand Léger, Albert Gleizes and Leopold Survage.*

pare proposals, and to make sure that the planned exhibition remain above all an artistic event open to all areas of creation:

> Not only architecture, sculpture, and painting . . . the art of the city and the country, but also music, lyrical drama, the dance, cinema, etc., and even eugenics, since the beauty of man, woman, and the child has always been one of the principal sources of inspiration for the plastic arts.[13]

But where the professed goal of the 1925 Exhibition had been founded on an ideology of progress through the application of art to industry, the ideals of the 1937 Exhibition were entirely different: Man instead of the machine was to be placed at the centre of the project:

> Every human creation needs a part of spiritual and sensible elements; 'Progress' conceived on the material level would lead civilization not to happiness, but to a scientifically structured barbarism, for Art, whether visible or hidden, is as necessary to Man as bread is to his body.[14]

Economic problems, changes in governments and a general lack of or-

254. Entrance to the Pavilion of the Société des artistes décorateurs, *1937 Exposition.*

ganization almost led to the abandonment of the exhibition project by December 1933. A reaction to the government's inertia took place on 5 February 1934, on the eve of the riots that would reveal the full extent of the social and political crisis facing the Republic, when the Union corporative de l'art français (UCAF), representing the major French artistic societies (Société des artistes décorateurs, Salon d'Automne, Société des artistes français), and the Federation des métiers d'art de France, announced that it would mount its own exhibition, even if the government refused support.[15] In response to growing pressure from these groups and from business and commercial interests, the newly-formed cabinet eventually reconsidered the Exhibition, and a new administrative body was set up in July 1934.[16] At the behest of the architect Pierre Montagnac, vice-president of the Société, the committee presented its project for the 1937 Exhibition before the Société's General Assembly in December 1935. It chose Pierre Patout (1879-1965), architect of Ruhlmann's *Pavillon d'un collectionneur* at the 1925 Exhibition, as the architect of the pavilion to be entitled *Maison de la Société*

256. Leonetto Cappiello, Poster for
the Exposition internationale des arts
et techniques dans la vie moderne, *1937.
Paris, musée de la Publicité.*

255. View of the Exposition of 1937
*from the Trocadéro. Left: German
Pavilion, Right: Soviet Pavilion.*

257. Suzanne Guiguichon,
Home for an Intellectual Couple.
*Pavilion of the Société
des artistes décorateurs, 1937.*

258. Emile Robert Lamy, Studio
of a Sculptor. *Pavilion of the Société
des artistes décorateurs, 1937.*

*259. Suzanne Guiguichon,
Home for an Intellectual Couple.
Pavilion of the Société
des artistes décorateurs, 1937.*

des artistes décorateurs. It was to be a luxurious town house, including reception rooms, private apartments, domestic quarters, kitchens and gymnasium, etc., in a spirit similar to the Société's "Embassy" of 1925. The pavilion would also house the official receptions given by the French government during the exhibition. But two members claiming to represent the younger faction of the Société, Maurice Barret and Etienne Kohlmann, objected that in the present economic circumstances the Société's efforts should be directed towards the community:

In our times, there can no longer be any important figures or large re-

ceptions such as we have just considered. This in no way interests our young people who see life from a simpler and more utilitarian side.[17] They submitted a counter-proposal for a model sports club in which artists could express themselves as they wished, and which would have special sections reserved for the various *corporations de métiers*—architects, ceramists, etc. In December 1935, resolving not to produce any excessively opulent interiors like the ones that had dominated its presentation in 1925, the Société voted on a compromise that would be entitled simply *La Maison des décorateurs*.[18]

*260. Maxime Old, Living-room.
Pavilion of the Société
des artistes décorateurs, 1937.*

*261. Alfred Porteneuve, Smoking-room.
Pavilion of the Société
des artistes décorateurs, 1937.*

The Paris Exposition internationale des arts et techniques dans la vie moderne opened on 24 May 1937. As in 1925, the pavilion of the Société was located in the main axis of the exhibition, at the heart of the *Centre des métiers*, a complex of buildings housing exhibits devoted to all of the French crafts. But the role of the Société in 1937 was not that of the champion of modernity in the decorative arts that it had been twelve years before; major modern design exhibits were housed in a special pavilion devoted to furnishings (in which many Société members exhibited individually), and in the pavilion of the Union des artistes modernes.
The Société's monumental three-storey pavilion, in reinforced concrete covered with plaques of fibro-ciment, crossed the neo-classical with International Style architecture, its horizontal aspect counterbalanced by four imposing buttresses enclosing elevators. Bas-reliefs representing the Arts and the Elements decorated the entrance to the otherwise hermetic façade. The four elevators took visitors directly to the third floor, where the tour of the individual stands began. Each floor had a particular atmosphere or theme: The third floor represented the "home of an

262. Jean Dunand, Les Biches dans une clairière, *lacquered panel shown in the* Smoking-room *by Alfred Porteneuve. Pavilion of the Société des artistes décorateurs, 1937.*

263. Alfred Porteneuve, Smoking-room. Pavilion of the Société des artistes décorateurs, 1937.

artist" and the "home of a doctor", the second floor featured luxury apartments, while the first floor offered group presentations, dominated by Jacques Adnet's *Weekend resort in the Ile-de-France*, and André Arbus' *Residence in the Ile-de-France*. The ground floor housed a reading room and information services.

Not less than 185 artists took part in the decoration of the pavilion. Many approaches and styles were repres-

ented, as well as several new themes directed towards youth, sports, and community and intellectual life. These themes had become central to the exhibition as a whole with the advent of the Popular Front's emphasis on cultural and physical enrichment. Suzanne Guiguichon presented a modern *Home for an intellectual couple*, where the living and sleeping areas were separated only by bookshelves, low, comfortable chairs, and elegant built-in

264. *Etienne Kohlmann*, Interior
of a Mountain Chalet. *Pavilion of the Société
des artistes décorateurs, 1937.*

Right page:

266. *Etienne-Henri Martin*, Boudoir,
*Pavilion of the Société
des artistes décorateurs, 1937.*

265. *Jacques Adnet*, Commons Room
for a Week-End Centre in the Ile-de-France.
*Pavilion of the Société
des artistes décorateurs, 1937.*

267. *André Arbus,* Dining-room
for a Residence in the Ile-de-France,
*Pavilion of the Société
des artistes décorateurs, 1937.
Cabinet in tortoise shell and gilt bronze,
glass panel by Paule Ingrand.*

268. *André Arbus,* Woman's Bedroom
for a Residence in the Ile-de-France,
*Pavilion of the Société
des artistes décorateurs, 1937.*

269. *André Arbus,* Music Room for
a Residence in the Ile-de-France,
*Pavilion of the Société
des artistes décorateurs, 1937.*

Following double page:

270. *André Arbus,* Divan *shown
in the* Woman's Bedroom *in the* Residence
in the Ile-de-France, *Pavilion of the Société
des artistes décorateurs, 1937.
Parchment and gold lacquer.
Paris, galerie Arc-en-Seine.*

271. *André Arbus,* Armchair, *lacquered wood,
embroidery after cartoons by Philippe Hosiasson.
Musée d'Art moderne de la Ville de Paris.
This model, with dark silk upholstery,
was shown in the* Music Room
by Arbus in Pavilion of the Société
des artistes décorateurs, 1937.

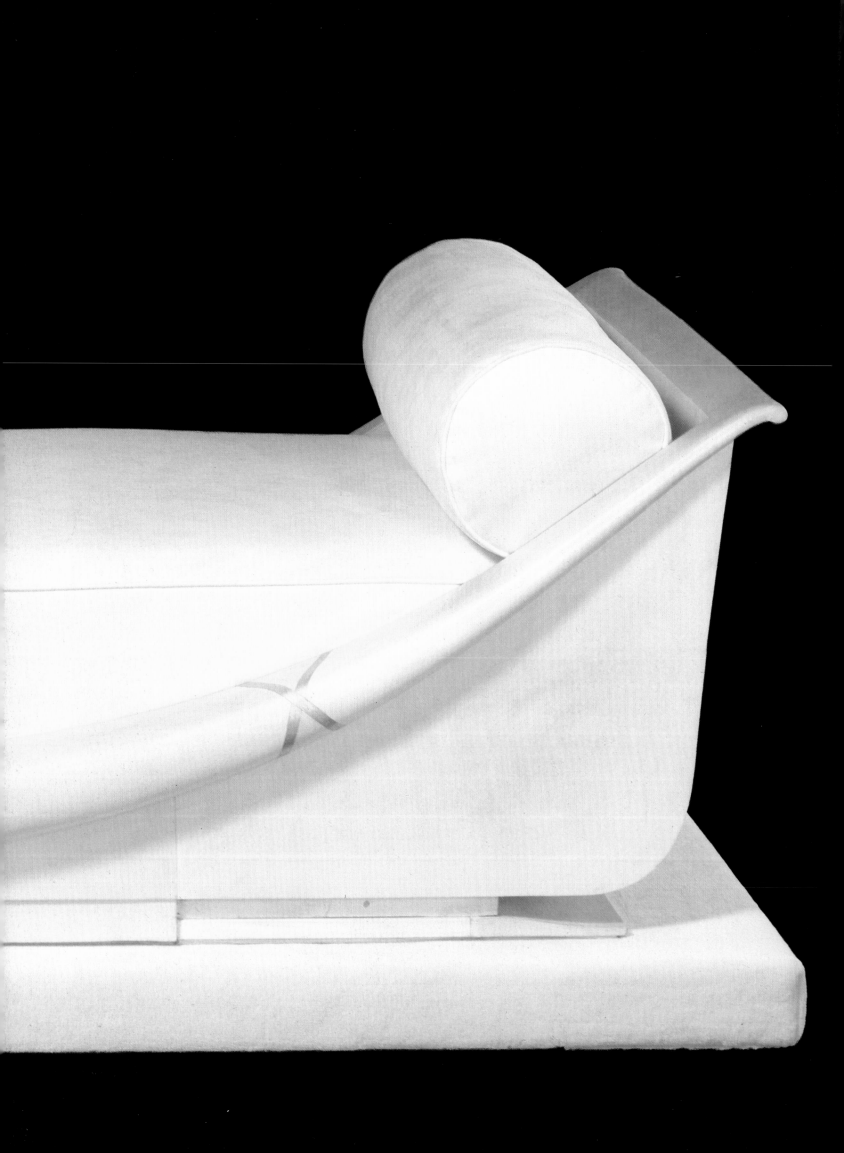

272 and 273. Louis Süe, Dining-room for an Embassy. *Pavilion of the Société des artistes décorateurs, 1937.*

274. *Louis Süe,* Drawing for a Vestibule of an Embassy, *1937. Louis Süe archives, Paris, Institut français d'architecture.*

275. *Louis Süe,* Music Corner for an Embassy. *Pavilion of the Société des artistes décorateurs, 1937. Louis Süe archives, Paris, Institut français d'architecture.*

276. *Maurice Dufrène,* Woman's Bedroom. *Designed for La Maîtrise. Pavilion of the Société des artistes décorateurs, 1937.*

277. *Louis Süe, Detail of the Dining-room*
of an Embassy, 1937.
Louis Süe archives.
Paris, Institut français d'architecture.

278. *Louis Süe,* Dining-room for
an Embassy. *Gouache on paper.*
Pavilion of the Société
des artistes décorateurs, 1937.
Louis Süe archives.
Paris, Institut français d'architecture.

279. A Street at Night, *Salon des Artistes décorateurs et de la Lumière, 1939.*
Chaise longue by Louis Sognot.
Louis Süe archives.
Institut français d'architecture.

wood furniture. The sober furnishings and dark tonalities of the *Sculptor's Studio* by E. Lamy attested to a new vision of the artist not as a decadent bohemian, but as an eminently rational assembler of forms. André Domin contributed a *Young woman's room for a university club*, and the theme of student life was also treated by Lucien Rollin and Gabriel Englinger. Sports and outdoor life were the subjects of several artists: Pierre Petit, in his *Hunting and Fishing Lodge*, sculpted a large oval space with walls of glass brick, terracotta floor tiles, and elegant armchairs in tubular steel with woven rush seating. Etienne Kohlmann presented an *Interior for a Mountain Chalet.*

The second floor of sumptuous interiors, entered through a monumental wrought-iron door by Raymond Subes, included the *Commons room in the l'Ile de France* by Jacques Adnet. A great circular fireplace stood in the centre of the room, and four high-backed chairs covered in black and white calf-skin surrounded a large table illuminated by red candles. The adjoining *Music Room* and *Woman's bedroom* forming part of the *Residence in the Ile-de-France* by André Arbus were large Manneristic spaces, at once neo-classical and surrealist, in which each element seemed imbued with special meaning by its isolation and special placement: a divan covered in

280. A Street at Night, *Salon of the artistes décorateurs in conjunction with the Salon de la Lumière, 1939.*

281. A Street at Night, *Salon of the artistes décorateurs in conjunction with the Salon de la Lumière, 1939.*

1931-1942

282. Jean-Denis Malclès, Cover for the Catalogue of the XXIXe Salon des artistes décorateurs et de la lumière.

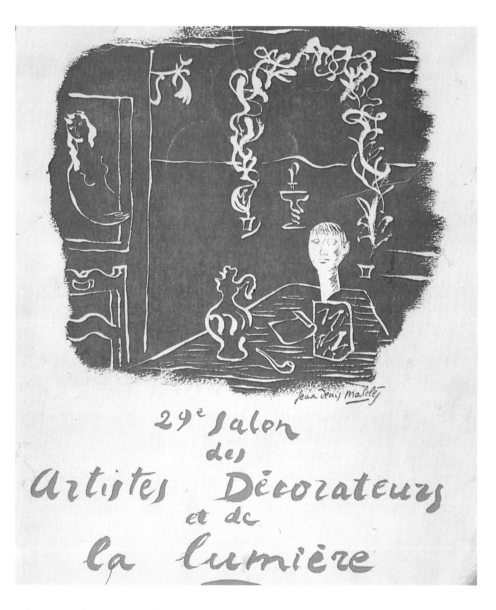

29e Salon des Artistes Décorateurs et de la lumière

283. Raoul Dufy, Poster. Paris, musée de la Publicité.

white parchment stood in a niche surmounted by a bird perched on floating drapery; musical instruments were carefully and deliberately set against the walls or on tables. Louis Süe took a similar approach in his *Embassy reception room*, crowded with mermaid-caryatids, balustrades, obelisks, yellow and white draperies, a divan covered in purple satin, and a candelabra in silvered glass with black candles. Even Maurice Dufrène joined this theatrical trend in his *Woman's*

bedroom, with a bed in gilded metal resting on glass balls, topped with a canopy of suspended draperies in red and green satin.

In his introduction to the pavilion's catalogue, Anatole de Monzie (1876-1947), then president of the Société, celebrated the demise of "architectural nudism" and the functionalism of the "iron age", lauding the return to more humanistic values and the renewed appreciation of noble materials: "The right to individualism in

284. Jacques Adnet, Gallery, 1939.
Glass brick by Saint-Gobain.

285. Louis Süe, Plan of the Salon
des artistes décorateurs
and the Salon de la Lumière, *1939.*

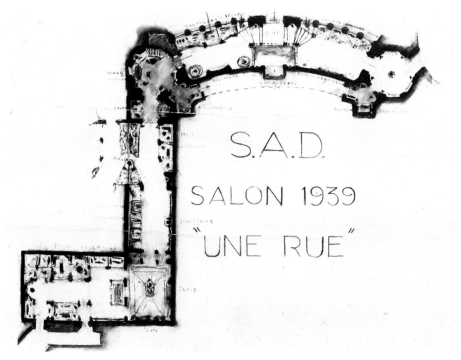

286. Marie-Madeleine Claude-Salvy,
Boutique de frivolités, 1939.

art is being reborn everywhere and with it a new taste for beautiful objects—the sign of spiritual freedom."[19] Some of the critics were disturbed, however, by the theatrical aspect of the interiors presented by Arbus, Dufrène and Süe. Critic Louis Cheronnet asked whether this reaction against the *affreux nudisme* of functionalist design had not opened the door to a refuge in the baroque:

> I am especially worried about seeing a reaction set in against the puritanical rigours of functionalism (rigours which were probably exaggerated, since they themselves provoked the reaction), one drawn from a mixture of neo-Humanism, folklore, and an antiquarian love of knick-knacks. . . . We should be careful of getting excited over small matters, of losing our footing on the path of sure and constant values because we are suddenly attracted by the ostentatiousness of appearances. The notion of humanity goes beyond the search for an aesthetics of adornment ; it must be subjected to an ethic whose demands are always linked to reality.[20]

287. *Louis Süe*, Bedroom, 1939.

This mannerist tendency that began to surface in 1937 emerged in an astounding fashion at the 1939 Salon, the Société's last before the war. Partially sponsored by the Compagnie parisienne d'éléctricité, the Salon was established in cooperation with the Salon de la lumière. Louis Süe, the new vice-president of the Société, was in charge of the general organization of the Salon, based on the theme of a *Street at night*. The exhibit incorporated the latest artistic and technological research in artificial lighting, here designed by Man Ray and the lighting engineers Jean Dourgnon and André Salomon, into an array of streets, boutiques, and domestic interiors constructed inside the Grand Palais. The Salon's overall aspect was undoubtedly influenced by the surrealist decors presented in the Pavillon d'Elégance at the 1937 Exposition, and the Exposition internationale du surréalisme, held at the Galerie des Beaux-Arts in Paris in 1938. Visitors were plunged into darkness as they entered the Salon through a circular hall containing metal sculptures representing the Arts, and illuminated with black light by Colette Gueden, director of the Printemps' Primavera studio. In the section intended to represent a street, Süe tried to recreate the ambiance of Venice at night in a fantasy cityscape composed of a *Theatre of dreams*, and walkways and bridges spanning a *Marvellous River* of shimmering paper. Jacques Adnet created an arcade of illuminated glass bricks and black glass columns manufactured by St. Gobain. Some of the most striking individual displays were by women. Decorator Claude-Salvy designed a *Boutique de frivolités* in which the merchandise (shoes, handbags and jewellery) could not be distinguished from the display itself—a romantico-surrealist world of truncated bodies and detached hands lit by an automatic mechanism that alternately

simulated night and daylight. Colette Gueden presented a *Table de parade*: a glass dining table set with dishes, candlesticks, and a tablecloth decorated with biomorphic motifs; the table seemed to hover in the air through special multicolour lighting effects. Louis Süe designed what can only be described as a caricature of a bedroom framed by a proscenium of carved

plaster draperies, with bold volumes played off against equally bold colours: the sculpted wood bed frame was painted green and white, the blue-green bed cover was trimmed with white braid, while the window was brilliantly illuminated with a beam of lemon yellow light. Still more suprising was the interior by Jean Royère: it had

288. Colette Guéden, Table de parade, *1939.*

289. Jean Royère, Salon, 1939.

290. Etienne-Henri Martin, Cabinet, 1939.

an orange ceiling and almond green and white walls. The brown carpet and white rug framed chairs upholstered in bright blue chintz with white dots that repeated the dappled effect of the orange-lacquered perforated zinc shades of a chandelier. A long divan and small chair covered with orange fabric were decorated with bands of fluffy white fur.

Writing in *Beaux-Arts*, S. Gille-Delafon was shocked by what he perceived as the lugubrious and decadent aspect of the Salon:

> This street that was announced to us did not have to be a real street, but we were not expecting it to be an attempt to perfect a decadent style.

There are astounding borrowings, an amazing Baroquism, superficial splendour, and vanity of detail. . . . O dear rigour, what have they done to you in this place? Serenity in the face of arms, we are told. Is it not, rather, an ignorance of the coming times? Papier-mâché optimism.[21]

In spite of the frivolous aspect of the Salon, in the shadow of war the majority of the press was able to admit its fascination with the exhibition. As one critic wrote:

> In this privileged place, the noise of the sick world does not reach us. It is, rather, devoted to joyful effort, to the pleasures of the eye, to spiritual peace. The Salon of the artistes

décorateurs is not only a demonstration of French taste, but even more, a testimonial to courage and optimism. What an oasis for all Parisians tired of hearing about 'vital space'![22]

The Occupation did not bring a halt to the activities of the Société des artistes décorateurs. Two Salons were held during the war: the first in the spring of 1940 together with the Salon d'Automne and the Salon des Tuileries, and the second in 1942. There is little information to document the Salons other than a list of the artists and the works exposed—the minutes of the Société's meetings stop in June 1939 and do not pick up again until September 1944. The existence of the Salons nevertheless demonstrates the sense of solidarity and corporate effort among the Société's members during these tragic years.

The war brought the end of an age in French design. The Société's project for a union between art and industry, never realized, ended in derision with the surrealist Salon of 1939. The project was resumed after the war, although this time it was based on a modified paradigm—one that would no longer equate modernity with social privilege, but which would eventually find, by necessity, a certain beauty in functionalism.

Suzanne Tise

291. Lucien Coutaud, La Pluie et le Beau Temps, *1941 (1942 Salon). Tapestry. Paris, galerie Yves Gastou.*

1931_____

12 May-11 July, Grand Palais

Catalogue cover: Lucien Derryx

Architects: Jean-François Meunier,
Henry Favier, Pierre Selmersheim,
Emile Aillaud, Pierre Montagnac,
Robert Henri, Léon Carrière,
Etienne Kohlmann

President: André Tardieu
Vice-presidents: Joseph Hiriart,
Paul Follot, André Frechet
General Secretary: Geo Lamothe
Secretaries: Paul Bablet, Etienne Kohlmann
Treasurer: René Kieffer

The Société's 1931 Salon lacked the splendour of the previous Salons; the effects of the economic crisis were already being felt, and many Société members were devoting most of their resources to their participation in the Exposition Coloniale, where they contributed an installation in the Palais des beaux-arts. At the Salon, a large section was devoted to sculpture, usually permitted at the Société only in a decorative capacity, and a small retrospective was held in honour of the sculptor Joseph Bernard. In general, the ensembles lacked the decorative exuberance of those immediately following the 1925 Exhibition, and the Cubist influence had all but disappeared. Forms were heavier, and lines were sober and more curved—as in the *Private Office* designed by Paul Follot. A few decorators continued to work with modern materials. René Gabriel used tubular steel in his *Hall*, and Djo-Bourgeois produced a set of garden furniture in cement and glass.

292. Gabriel Englinger, Child's Bedroom.

293. Djo-Bourgeois, Garden table.
Cement and glass.

294. Léon and Maurice Jallot, Waiting area.

295. Paul Follot, Corner of a private office.

296. René Gabriel, Waiting room in a hall.

1932

4 May-9 July, Grand Palais

President: André Tardieu
Vice-presidents: Joseph Hiriart,
Paul Follot, André Fréchet
General Secretary: Geo Lamothe
Secretaries: Etienne Kohlmann,
Jean Mayodon
Treasurer: Pierre Montagnac

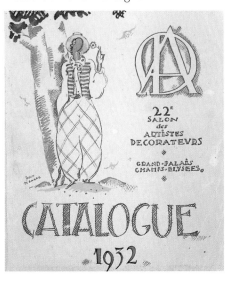

297. Jean Debarre, Catalogue cover.

298. Maurice Daurat, Bowl. Hammered pewter.

The minutes from the meetings of the Société show that numerous members experienced serious unemployment problems when the economic crisis hit the building and decoration industries in 1931.[23] Conservative spokesmen for the various crafts associations blamed these difficulties on increasing mechanization and an excessive use of new materials like concrete and metal that eliminated the possibility of fine craftsmanship.

A lament over the loss of artistic traditions also can be found in the curious introduction to the 1932 Salon catalogue written by architect Joseph Hiriart, then vice-president of the Société, in which he described the young woman on the catalogue cover as the symbol of the designers' return to French tradition after a decade of confusion:

They [artists] have been tossed about by these mad times born of the great cataclysm. From Moscow to New York, from Asia to Africa, the storms have devastated the landscapes where before, in the ages of Faith, harmonious and spiritual works were erected. . . . Inspiration has ceased to exist, common faith is absent, the collective spirit that spawned our great national works has been extinguished. Would it disappear forever, this inspiration that created our cathedrals and castles, that of Jean-Jacques and Hernani? Thay have suffered and they have sinned, and by their suffering, how many sins have been redeemed! In visiting my great Salon, you will discover in the works displayed the first rays of the great sun rising again over the French tradition regained.[24]

Indeed, there was a striking return to fine craftsmanship at the 1932 Salon. Tubular steel and the machine aesthetic were almost entirely absent in furniture; wood and heavier, more curved forms predominated. One of the most impressive changes in style could be found in Ruhlmann's *Rendez-vous de pêcheurs,* where his habitual sense of elegance was combined with a new interest in rusticity and the picturesque. Lucien Rollin presented a *Dining-room* and woman's *Boudoir* in violet wood that expressed a classic sophistication, and employed a wide range of materials and fine craftsmanship: engraved mirrors by Max Ingrand, forged ironwork by Gilbert Poillerat, and tapestries designed by André Mare and executed by Aubusson.

299. Raymond Subes, Door designed for the Church of Saint-Pierre de Roye. Forged iron.

300. Lucien Rollin, Dining-room.
Mahogany, tapestry executed by Aubusson
after cartoons by André Mare,
console in forged iron by Gilbert Poillerat,
lighting by Jean Perzel.

301. Lucien Rollin, Boudoir. Violet wood,
engraved glass by Max Ingrand
from designs by Paule Ingrand.

1933 _____

5 May-9 July, Grand Palais

Catalogue cover: Jean-Denis Malclès

Organization of Salon: Georges Beau,
Maurice Jallot, Henri Rapin,
Lucie Renaudot, Louis Süe

President: André Tardieu
Vice-presidents: Pierre Montagnac,
Adolphe Dervaux, Raymond Subes
General Secretary: Geo Lamothe
Secretaries: Jean Luce, Maurice Jallot
Treasurer: René Kieffer

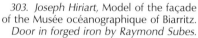

303. Joseph Hiriart, Model of the façade
of the Musée océanographique of Biarritz.
Door in forged iron by Raymond Subes.

Left page:

302. Djo-Bourgeois, Exposition Hall.
*Sculptures by Léon Leyritz,
decorative panel by Pierre Lardin.*

304. Jacques Adnet, Living-room. *Cabinet
and chair covered in white goat-skin.*

305. René Prou, Living-room for
a Villa on the Côte-d'Azur.

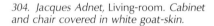

Some commentators on the economic
crisis and the unemployment that had
reached epic proportions by 1933 believed
that the situation was the fault of a civilization that relegated the individual to a
secondary position and attributed too
much importance to material wealth.
Paradoxically, in the case of the decorative
arts, this new attention to humanism
centred on the question of the human
need for ornament. The review *Art et
Décoration* considered the issue so important that it opened an inquiry "Evolution ou mort de l'ornement?" in April 1933,
to which the critic Waldemar George replied:

> The ideal of material comfort and utilit-
> arianism to the exclusion of all other
> ideals, attests to a state of barbarism
> without precedent in the history of art.
> If a work must be useful by an exact
> adaptation to its function, the confusion
> between the useful and the beautiful

306. Eugène Printz, Living-room.

*307. Jean-Denis Malclès,
Catalogue cover.*

*308. Jean Luce, Table Service.
Faïence. Paris, galerie Suger.*

Right page:

*309. Jules Leleu, Floor lamp, 1933.
Paris, galerie Arc-en-Seine.*

310. Jules Leleu, Living-room.

can only lead to misunderstandings. The civilization whose architecture and decorative arts bore the stamp of the UAM [Union des artistes modernes] and the Bankhaus [sic] of Dessau has ended in total failure. Architecture and the decorative arts must now be founded on a more human, concrete and sensible basis. It is not a matter of choosing a new style, but of a new contact with things, a new harmony and a new ethic.[25]

It was in the midst of this debate that the 23rd Salon of the artistes décorateurs

opened in 1933. Critic Gaston Derys praised the return to the traditional crafts of decorative painting and tapestry, and the "humanisation" of metal furnishings, like those of René Prou's *Dining-room for a Villa on the Cote d'Azur* in lacquered red forged *duralumin,* or in the decorative bronze pedastal employed by Eugène Printz in the cabinet presented in his *Living-room*:

Decor! We shall not revive here this bitter controversy. Ornament: should it be condemned forever or should we hope for its renaissance? . . . Here is a

religion that is losing its followers. This reversal of opinion was fatal in any case. Whether we like it or not, ornament is part of human nature. It cannot be excluded from the works of man, but it must never be used arbitrarily. . . . Another observation: tubular furniture has definitely been abandoned. Metal furniture is losing ground. There is, by the way, some charming country furniture in metal. Metal for the country, for the office, for public installations, what could be more rational? The counter-attack of wood is undeniable.[26]

1934

311. Georges Lepape, Catalogue cover.

4 May-8 July, Grand Palais

Catalogue cover: Georges Lepape

Architecture: Pierre Selmersheim

President: Joseph Hiriart
Vice-presidents: Pierre Montagnac,
Adolphe Dervaux, Raymond Subes
Secretaries: Jean Mayodon, André Marty
General Secretary: Geo Lamothe
Treasurer: René Kieffer

312. Albert Guénot, Petit Salon/Boudoir.
Designed for La Pomone.

313. Jacques Adnet, Salon/Studio.
Designed for Mr. and Mrs. Jay Gould.

315. *Jean Perzel,* Lamp *shown in the* Bedroom *by Lucien Rollin.*

314. *Lucien Rollin,* Bedroom. *Walnut, lighting by Jean Perzel.*

The widespread belief among those associated with the decorative arts that the disappearance of ornament would naturally lead to the disappearance of craftsmanship placed the members of the Société in a difficult situation. Though caught in the grip of the depression, they were artists, and would continue to create. Commissions, however, were rare. In 1932 the city of Paris had promised the Société that it would try to provide opportunities for some decorators through large-scale, public decoration projects, but these had not materialized. Commissions for the interiors of the luxurious oceanliner *Normandie* provided possibilities for an elite of artists, many from the Société, but hundreds of others remained without work. They were thus forced to count on work from a small cultivated elite of Parisian society, and this is why, in spite of the atmosphere of crisis, luxurious ensembles such as the *Salon* designed by Jacques Adnet for Mr. and Mrs. Jay Gould could be presented at the 1934 Salon. At the same time, the virulent attacks against "nudism" in furnishings was increasingly associated with foreign influences by a reactionary press, and corporative associations that saw their livelihood threatened by the clean lines and smooth surfaces of the modern design injected patriotism into the question of style. There was a distinct tendency at the Salon to try to find modern applications for a broad range of traditional crafts, and we find stylistic references, though somewhat updated, to the French tradition. While the reviews devoted to the decorative arts (largely supported by advertisements bought by the decoration and building industries), commended the new vitality of the Salon, J.P. Sabatou, one of the editors of *Architecture d'Aujourd'hui*, was disturbed by the inclination to consider nationalism a factor in the creation of art, and the attention being paid to unneeded ornament and handicraft rather than to more pertinent questions of functionalism and economy. He wrote in his review of the 1934 Salon:

This year we can see the first consequences of the artistic nationalism which, for some time, and in every country, has been violently tormenting spirits. Each boasts of a national art and architecture that owes nothing to the others, and finds strength and beauty only in itself. This is all well and good, but before blindly running off in a new direction, it would be prudent to know where it leads and if the momentum behind these new directives does indeed possess the faith and passion that ennoble artistic endeavours—even if they are mistakes—or, on the contrary, if art in this adventure is only a pretext; it all being, at bottom, a matter of money. . . . The result, for this time it is tangible, is that we risk falling into a materialism, a vulgarity that will no doubt please a public that has been deluded and exploited. In the space of a few short years, the public has been forced to abandon decorative romanticism and accept the nudity of steel tubes, only to be faced today with the ornaments and embellishments whose uselessness it had just begun to understand. And why? The mouldings, the rows of beads *à la moderne*, the studs, the sculptures tacked on or carved from the block (as on a Henri II sideboard), will they save the crafts, give work to artists and men of good will, dethrone machinism, or help us overcome this crisis? The crisis at this Salon is not material, but spiritual; it lacks a direction and an ideal.[27]

1935

3 May-14 July, Grand Palais

President: André Tardieu
Vice-presidents: Joseph Hiriart,
Raymond Subes, Louis Bonnier
General Secretary: Geo Lamothe
Secretaries: André Marty, Jean Mayodon
Treasurer: René Kieffer

The Salon of 1935 was something of a reversal of the Salons of the preceding years. In spite of calls for a return to tradition, many ensembles reflected contemporary concerns with health, hygiene, outdoor life and the democratization of sports. In addition, the more practical, even rustic atmosphere of the Salon contrasted greatly with the lavish interiors created by many Société members for the oceanliner Normandie, launched in 1935.

The majority of the interiors displayed nothing of the theatrical spaces that had so impressed the visitors to previous Salons. Several designers returned to tubular steel, and there was a greater sense of horizontality in the design of ensembles, evoking a more relaxed lifestyle, as in the

Terrace for a Parisian Apartment Building by Colette Geuden. Furniture was low to the ground or built into the walls. Natural materials and blond woods prevailed in what the press dubbed a "rustic modernism". One of the most successful interiors of this kind was the *Studio* by Suzanne Guiguichon, designed for the ideal young man of the 1930s—who was both athletic and intellectual. This was suggested not only by the sports photographs over the desk, but also by the simple, rational and unencumbered furnishings combining polished oak, thick, undyed wools and raw linen. Maurice Barret contributed one of the most controversial interiors, making extensive use of metal for the furnishings as well as other modern

*316. Maurice Barret,
Studio for an intellectual worker.
Furnishings in standardized metal elements.*

317. *Colette Gueden,*
Terrace for an apartment building in Paris.
Designed for Primavera.

318. *Pierre Petit,* Ensemble
Repos Côte-d'Azur.

319. Marie Lemaistre, Child's Playroom.

materials such as glass brick and sound-proof wall coverings—a courageous move in the climate of hostility towards functionalism. His *Chambre d'un travailleur intellectuel* measured 25 m² and contained a sophisticated system of standardized storage units intended to keep the small space free of clutter. He described his approach to interior design in an article published in *Le Décor d'Aujourd'hui* in 1935:

Since I have been allowed to defend my work here, I would say first of all that it is not 'my' work, but a 'collective' work. For the first time, the *architecte-décorateur* has attempted a total collaboration with industry. For the first time he has abandoned his power as

'creator' for a new role: that of 'master of ceremonies'. . . . From now on, this world will be the result of collective efforts in which the industrialist, the technician, the organizer, etc., will co-operate with the creator-designer of forms and objects. The entire Salon—with a few exceptions—stands in opposition to this principle. Each is a 'dictator'; the technician is simply an executant. Poor little dictator with clay feet, the technical progress of machinism will sweep you aside soon enough, you and your 'art', if you do not learn how to adapt and to react in a positive and joyous way, instead of whining over machines and crying over 'lost art, broken sensitivity, etc.' . . .²⁹

1936

6 May-5 July, Grand Palais

Organization of Salon:
Pierre Selmersheim, Raymond Subes,
Paul Bablet, Maurice Daurat

President: André Tardieu
Vice-presidents: Pierre-Paul Montagnac,
Louis Bonnier, André Marty
General Secretary: Geo Lamothe
Secretaries: Etienne Kohlmann,
Gilbert Poillerat
Treasurer: Jean Luce

320. *Jacques Adnet*, Study for an Art Lover.
Bleached Oak, lamp by Jean Perzel.

321. *Andre Arbus*, Young Girl's Bedroom.
*Furniture covered in white parchment,
fabrics by Paule Marrot.*

322. *Albert Guénot*, Dining-room.

The Salon of 1936 was dominated by the
"humanized rationalism" that had developed at the previous Salon. Etienne
Kohlmann, Suzanne Guiguichon, Albert
Guenot, and Maxime Old presented ensembles dominated by a concern with the
organization of space and simple, economical furnishings in natural materials.
Another group of designers introduced
Surrealism into the domestic interior, as in
the display of floral fabrics by Paule Marrot,
and the theatrical *Boudoir blanc de
Rosalinde* by Marie-Madeleine Claude-
Salvy.[29]

1936 _____

323. *Marie-Madeleine Claude-Salvy,*
Boudoir Blanc de Rosalinde.
Furniture in white lacquer,
forged iron and glass.
Decorative panel by Madeleine Lucas.

324. Maxime Old, Reclining Chair.

1938 _____

7 May-10 July, Grand Palais

President: Anatole de Monzie
Vice-presidents: Pierre Paul Montagnac,
Louis Bonnier, René Keiffer
General Secretary: Geo Lamothe
Secretaries: André Arbus, Jean Dunand
Treasurer: René Gabriel

326. *René Gabriel,* Dining-room.

327. *Maurice Pré,* Rocking chair.

328. *Maxime Old,* Dining-room.
Canadian birch.

325. *René Gabriel,* Studio/Dining-room. *Ash.*

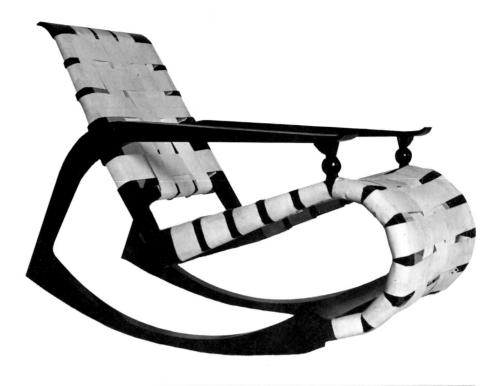

1939

10 May-14 July, Grand Palais, in conjunction with the Salon de la Lumière

President: Anatole de Monzie
Vice-presidents: Louis Süe, Urbain Cassan, Raymond Subes
Administrative Secretary: Ulysse Crétois
Secretaries: André Arbus, Jacques Adnet
Treasurer: René Kieffer

329. A Street at Night.

330. *Suzanne Guiguichon*, Bedroom.

The Salon was divided into eight groups, each with an artistic director:

Group A: Urbain Cassan

Group B: Jacques Adnet
Lighting designer: Louis Touchagues
Ingénieur-éclairagiste: André Salomon

Group C: Louis Süe
Lighting Designer: Louis Touchagues

Group D: Jules Leleu
Architect: Paul Tournon
Lighting Designer: Louis Touchagues
Ingénieur-éclairagiste: André Salomon

Group E: Alfred Porteneuve
Lighting Designer: Jean Dourgnon
Assistant: Paul Bonet

Group F: Louis Süe, Colette Gueden
Lighting designer: Man Ray
Ingénieur-éclairagiste: St. Grebel

Group G: Louis Süe
Lighting designer: Man Ray
Ingénieur-éclairagiste: St. Grebel

Group H: André Arbus
Lighting designers: Vigneau, Jean Dourgnon
Ingénieur-éclairagiste: St. Grebel

The Société's 29th Salon opened only a little more than a week after Hitler made his response to Roosevelt's propositions for peace, and as England was arming itself for war. Yet nothing of these terrible realities could be seen in the Société's 1939 Salon presented in cooperation with the Salon de la Lumière—it was a surrealist fantasy world on the theme of "A Street at Night".[30] In the introduction to the catalogue, the committee attempted to justify the huge discrepancy between the tragic events unfolding in the "real world" and the magical dream world that the designers had created in the galleries of the Grand Palais:

Why this street which is not a street? Indeed, it has no sidewalks, no pedestrian crossings and its only signs are from the realm of fantasy. These houses are not real houses, and we have not tried to make them real. If everything in this Salon is conventional, it is because convention is the shortest path to the truth, and these evocations of squares, gardens, churches, theatre façades, bridges and rivers, are only pretexts for us to create life though discipline, by subjecting fantasy to a rigour of scale and coordinating our efforts, to place painting and sculpture in their true architectural contexts: all these are things that we find healthy and creative. It may be necessary to remind you that this Salon was conceived amidst the threat and thunder of war. We are proud to say that you will find here only a demonstration of our serenity. The news reports and alarms of the outside world have vanished at our doorstep. The language we speak is a language of optimism. It is that of the France of the engineers and gardeners, of the workshops and forges. The doors of this street open onto dwellings whose inhabitants believe more than ever in the virtue of spiritual values.[31]

331. André Arbus, Summer Room, *fabrics by Paule Marrot.*

332. Michel Dufet, Bedroom.

Notes

The notes preceded by an asterisk correspond to the sections written by Yvonne Brunhammer.

1900-1914

1. *Procès-verbal de la première réunion de la Société des artistes décorateurs*, 7 February 1901. The *procès-verbaux* referred to throughout the text, presently housed in the archives of the Société des artistes décorateurs in Paris, have not been catalogued. The names of the other nine founders are not mentioned in the minutes of the first meeting, which took place in the Café du Gaz, rue de Rivoli.

2. Here I refer to those artists and draftsmen who designed furnishings and objects, the ornaments that decorated them, or decorative schemes for interiors (wall decorations, mosaics, etc.).

3. *Procès-verbal de la réunion du comité de la Société des artistes décorateurs*, May 1901.

4. Siegfried Bing's pavilion at the Exposition of 1900 was an exception in the French section. On Bing, see Gabriel P. Weisberg, *Art Nouveau Bing, Paris Style 1900*, New York, Abrams, 1986. On the German section at the Exposition, see Exposition universelle de 1900, *Catalogue officiel de la section allemande*, Berlin, 1900. Because of political tensions, Germany was not officially invited to participate at the Exposition universelle of 1900—the displays were organized on private initiative. This was the first time that the general public in France had been confronted with extensive German industrial and commercial power, although the French government had been observing the progress of the German applied art reform movement since the 1880s. See for example Marius Vachon, *Pour la défense de nos industries d'art: L'instruction artistique des ouvriers en Allemagne, Angleterre, et en Autriche. Missions officielles d'enquête.* Paris, Lahure, 1899.

5. On the history of the Munich Werkstätten, see Katheryn Bloom Hiesinger, *Art Nouveau in Munich, Masters of Jugendstil*, exhibition catalogue, Philadelphia Museum of Art, 1988.

6. According to the Werkstätten's aims, made public in January 1898, its goals were economic and nationalistic as well as aesthetic. See Heisinger, p. 12.

7. This was already a problem in the 1880s, and was decribed in a government inquiry into the decorative arts begun in 1881. See in particular the testimony of the cabinet-maker Séné in *Commission d'enquête sur la situation des ouvriers et des industries d'art*, Direction des beaux-arts, Paris, 1884, p. 311.

8. Parisian manufacturers would even complain to the City Council that after the Exhibition of 1900 they were apparently left with large stocks of Art Nouveau-style furnishings that they could not sell. See discussion in Conseil municipal de Paris, *Procès-verbaux*, 1912, Paris 1913, n° 1782, p. 1018. On Art Nouveau and the applied arts reform movement in France during the second half of the 19th century, see Debora Silverman, *Nature, Nobility and Neurology, the Ideological Origins of Art Nouveau*, Ph.D. dissertation, Princeton University, 1983.

9. Frantz Jourdain, "Les meubles et les tentures murales aux salons de 1901", *Revue des arts décoratifs*, vol. 21, 1901, p. 212.

10. René Guilleré, *Projet pour une Société nationale des arts décoratifs*, Paris, 1900, p. 5.

11. The decorative arts came under the authority of the Ministry of Commerce.

12. Guilleré, p. 10. The Comte de Laborde (1807-1869) was the official reporter for the French government at the London Great Exhibition of 1851. His study on the situation of the French decorative arts, "De l'union des arts à l'industrie", published in 1856, launched the applied arts reform movement in France.

13. Document conserved in the Archives of the Société des artistes décorateurs.

14. On Dubufe see Emmanuel Bréon, *Claude-Marie, Edouard et Guillaume Dubufe, Portraits d'un siècle d'élégance parisienne*, Paris, Délégation de l'Action artistique de la Ville de Paris, 1987.

15. Only unique, hand-crafted objects were permitted; industrially manufactured objects were excluded. Marie Jeannine Aquilino has recently shown how Dubufe, in his interior installations for the salon of the Société nationale des beaux-arts, paid unprecedented attention to the grouping and coherent placement of artworks. He was also careful to make the Salon environment appealing to a new consumer public by designing luxurious spaces decorated with tapestries, carpets, draperies and potted plants. See her discussion in "The Decorating Campaigns at the Salon du Champ-de-Mars and the Salon des Champs-Elysées in the 1890s", *Art Journal*, vol. 48, Spring 1989, pp. 78-84.

16. Bréon, p. 223.

17. *Bulletin de la Société des artistes décorateurs*, April 1902, p. 8.

18. *Procès-verbal du comité de la Société des artistes décorateurs*, 11 December 1901. See also discussion in *Bulletin de la Société des artistes décorateurs*, April 1902.

19. *Bulletin du Comité de la Société des artistes décorateurs*, 1902, report by Edme Couty.

20. See discussion in *Bulletin de la Société des artistes décorateurs*, April 1902, pp. 27-37.

21. For example, in December 1901, the Société refused membership to jeweller Henri Véver because he was considered more of a commercial manufacturer than an *artiste-créateur*. See the *Procès-verbal du Comité de la Société des artistes décorateurs*, 18 December 1901.

22. *Procès-verbal du Comité de la Société des artistes décorateurs*, 11 December, 1901.

23. *Bulletin de la Société des artistes décorateurs*, 1902, p. 38.

24. It is interesting to note that soon after this decision was made, Rupert Carabin resigned from the Société, and Eugène Grasset and Bellery-Desfontaines resigned from the committee. Grasset returned briefly in 1903, and resigned a second time just before the first salon of the Société in 1904. *Procès-verbal du Comité de la Société des artistes décorateurs*, 23 April and 21 May 1902; 3 November 1904.

25. The programme was announced as follows: "This salon should be conceived as a sort of street-front boutique, with two outer façades on a corner, and which could be installed on the ground floor of a building in Paris. . . . It should include a common room and one or more small salons able to hold at least six people." *Art et Décoration*, supplément, May 1902, p. 6.

26. In creating the section of rustic art, the Société wanted to "display the creations of peasants, which have been disdained until now by industrial exhibitions in favour of objects of false luxury which are often less sincere". See "Chronique des arts et de la curiosité", supplement to *Gazette des Beaux-Arts*, n° 23, 7 June 1902, p. 178.

27. *Procès-verbal de l'Assemblée générale de la Société des artistes décorateurs*, 3 November 1908.

28. This was the opinion of Camille Mauclair, "Où en est notre art décoratif", *Revue bleue*, 24 April 1909, pp. 520-521.

29. It was only during the second half of the 1890s, and in the context of discussions on an "art for the people", that the ideas of William Morris began to be discussed in France. See for example the study by Jean Lahor (pseudonym for Doctor Henri Cazalis, 1840-1909) *L'art pour le peuple à défaut de l'art par le peuple*, Paris, 1902. Lahor, who considered himself the French William Morris, founded the Société internationale d'art et hygiène populaire in 1904, and was one of the organizers of the section "art rustique" at the 1904 Salon of the Société des artistes décorateurs.

30. Jean Laran, "Quelques meubles de Georges de Feure", *Art et Décoration*, July-December 1908, p. 124.

31. G.V. "La Course à l'abime", *Art et Industrie*, July, 1909, n.p.

32. Cited in Louis Vauxcelles, "L'Art décoratif au Salon d'automne", *Art et Industrie*, November, 1910, n.p.

33. Frantz Jourdain had been a partisan of decorative arts reform in France since the

1880s. Part of his goal in founding the Salon d'Automne in 1903 was to exhibit the decorative arts on an equal basis with the fine arts.

34. Cited in Otto Grautoff, "Die Münchner Austellung im Urteil Der Pariser Presse", *Dekorative Kunst*, 1910, p. 50.

35. Salon d'Automne, Paris, 1910, *Exposition des arts décoratifs de Munich*, Preface by Baron von Pechmann.

36. Cited in Grautoff, 54.

37. See Alphonse Deville, "Rapport au nom de la 4e commission sur les projets et pétitions relatifs à la date et au caractère de l'exposition (projetée) des arts décoratifs et des industries d'art", 1912, Archives Nationales, F21 4051.

38. René Guilleré, "Appel adressé par la Société des artistes décorateurs", *Catalogue du sixième Salon de la Société des artistes décorateurs*, 1911.

39. René Guilleré, *Rapport sur une exposition internationale des arts décoratifs modernes, Paris 1915*, Paris 1911, Archives François Carnot, bibliothèque des Arts décoratifs, Paris. This report was co-signed by the representatives of the Salon d'Automne, the Société de l'encouragement à l'art et à l'industrie, the Union centrale des arts décoratifs, and the Société nationale de l'art à l'école.

40. André Vera, "Le nouveau style", *L'Art Décoratif*, January 1912, p. 32.

41. An important precedent for such ensembles had already been set by Siegfried Bing in the gallery he opened on the rue de Provence in 1895.

42. The actress was a personal friend of René Guilleré. She was also an accomplished sculptor and a member of the Société, which she had been actively supporting since 1902. She even offered to let the Société set up a small exhibition in the entry hall of her theatre. *Procès-verbaux*, Comité de la Société des artistes décorateurs, 19 November 1902.

43. Clément-Janin, "Introduction", *Catalogue du premier salon de la Société des artistes décorateurs*, 1904.

44. *Assemblée Générale*, 17 June 1911.

45. Le Comité, "Appel adressé par la Société des artistes décorateurs", *Catalogue du Sixième Salon des artistes décorateurs*, 1911, pp. 6-7, and pp. 11-12.

In February 1911, the Comité of the Société obtained a promise from the Minister of Beaux-Arts, Dujardin-Beaumetz, that the state would make a greater number of purchases from decorative artists, and especially from creators of furniture. *Assemblée Générale*, 6 February 1911.

46. *Catalogue du septième salon de la Société des artistes décorateurs*, 1912, "Règlement du VIIe Salon", article III, p. 39. The former rule, more ambiguous as to the definition of "modern", read as follows: " . . . elle [the exhibition] est ouverte à toutes les manifestations d'art décoratif appliqué aux besoins modernes, sous la condition qu'elles seront des œuvres originales et surtout qu'elles tendront à créer de nouvelles formules décoratives." "Règlement", *Catalogue du premier Salon des artistes décorateurs*, 1904, p. 3.

47. Here, however, only the manufacturer's name was mentioned; the address and further information were provided after the object entry.

48. Louis Vauxcelles, "Le septième Salon des artistes décorateurs", *Art et Industrie*, April 1912, pp. 123-124.

49. See Francois Carnot, "Proposition de loi tendant à organiser en 1915, à Paris, une Exposition internationale des arts décoratifs modernes", 6 February 1912, typed manuscript, Archives Carnot, Paris, bibliothèque des Arts décoratifs.

50. His response was also published in *Le Figaro*, 14 December, 1912.

51. François Carnot, "Lettre ouverte à Monsieur Delville, président de la 4e commission du Conseil Municipal de Paris", *Catalogue du huitième salon de la Société des artistes décorateurs*, 1913, pp. 8-9.

52. The founder and president of the Société, René Guilleré, resigned in 1912 to organize the first decorative arts studio, Primavera, for Printemps department store. He was replaced by Henry Marcel, who served only briefly at the beginning of 1913 before being called to the direction of the Musées nationaux.

53. *Procès-verbal du Comité de la Société des artistes décorateurs*, May 1914.

54. Fernand Roches, "La question de l'art décoratif et notre temps, A propos du Salon des artistes décorateurs de 1914", *L'Art Décoratif*, June 1914, p. 175.

1919-1924

* 1. Léon Moussinac, *La Décoration théâtrale*, Paris, F. Rider et Cie., 1922, p. 50.

1. The notion of a *retour* or *rappel à l'ordre* has been the subject of several recent studies on French art during the interwar years. The term *rappel à l'ordre* was first employed by painter Roger Bissière in an article on an exhibition of paintings by Georges Braque held at the Galerie de l'Effort Moderne in 1919 published in *l'Opinion* 29 March and 26 April 1919. On the ramifications of the notion of a *retour à l'ordre* on post-war art in France see Jean Laude et al., *Le retour à l'ordre dans les arts plastiques et l'architecture*, Saint-Etienne, 1975; Kenneth E. Silver, *Esprit de Corps, The Art of the Parisian Avant-Garde and the First World War 1914-1925*, Thames and Hudson, London, 1989; and Christopher Green, *Cubism and its Enemies*, London, Yale, 1988; and Michel Collomb, *La Littérature art déco*, Paris, Meridiens Klincksieck, 1987.

2. André Vera, "La Doctrine décorative de demain", *Le Matin*, 21 November 1918. This essay was published in no less than four other reviews and journals during the following year: *La Grande Revue*, 1918, *La Belle France*, 1919, *Le Petit Messager*, 1919, *Les Arts Français*, 1919.

3. Vera, *Le Matin*, 21 November 1918.

4. Charles-Henri Besnard, "Les procédés modernes de construction rapide", *Art et Décoration*, January-June 1920, pp. 27-32.

5. The Société members known to have been mobilized in January 1915 were Edgar Brandt, Paul Follot, Mathieu Gallerey, Léon Jallot, Gustave Jaulmes, Emile Lenoble, Edouard Monod-Herzen, Henri Rapin, Tony Selmersheim, Louis Sézille, Adalbert Szabo, Georges Bourgeat. Paul Vitry, "Société des artistes décorateurs", *Le Petit Messager des Arts*, January 1915, p. 3.

6. *Procès-verbal de l'assemblée générale de la Société des artistes décorateurs*, 14 May 1919, p. 7.

7. Ibid, p. 7.

8. Ibid, p. 8.

9. Paul Vitry, "Introduction", *Catalogue du dixième Salon de la Société des artistes décorateurs*, Paris, 1919, p. 4.

10. On Süe and Mare see Susan Day, *Louis Süe, Architectures*, Mardaga, Liège and Brussels, 1986.

11. Léon Riotor, "Proposition relative à la participation de la Ville de Paris et du Departement de la Seine à l'Exposition internationale des arts décoratifs et industriels modernes en 1923", *Bulletin du Conseil Municipal*, n⁰ 71, 1920, p. 1.

12. Paul Vitry, "Avant-propos", *Catalogue du XIe Salon de la Société des artistes décorateurs*, 1920, pp. 3-4.

13. The term Art Deco, derived from the 1925 Exposition des arts décoratifs, was coined during the 1960s.

14. On the applied arts workshops of the Parisian department stores, see Suzanne Tise, "Les Grands Magasins", in *L'Art de Vivre, Decorative Arts and Design in France 1789-1989*, published on the occasion of an exhibition at the Cooper-Hewitt Museum, New York, 1989, pp. 73-106.

15. *Procès-verbal de l'Assemblée générale de la Société des artistes décorateurs*, 15 December 1922, p. 7.

16. Bokanowski was first elected to the Chamber of Deputies in 1914. In the early 1920s he was considered one of the few members of parliament to possess complete mastery of public finance and international economics. He was named Minister of the Navy in 1924, and then Minister of Commerce and Aeronautics in 1926. See Stephen A. Schuker, *The End of French Predominance in Europe*, Chapel Hill, 1976, p. 66.

17. *Procès-verbal de l'Assemblée générale de la Société des artistes décorateurs*, 6 November 1924.

18. "Le Salon des décorateurs", *L'Art et les artistes*, March-July, 1924, p. 394.

19. During 1923 and 1924 they were also working together on the decoration of the villa of the Viscount de Noailles, built by Robert Mallet-Stevens in Hyères.

20. See Elisabeth Hausser, *Paris au jour le jour, 1900-1919*, Paris 1968, Chapter 1919.

21. Paul Vitry, "Avant-propos", *Catalogue du Xe salon de la Société des Artistes décorateurs*, 1919, pp. 3-4.

22. Frantz Jourdain, "Avant-propos", *Catalogue du XVe salon de la Société des artistes décorateurs*, 1924, pp. 4-6.

1925

* 1. Roger Marx, "De l'art social et de la nécessité d'en assurer le progrès par une exhibition", *Idées modernes*, vol. 1, January 1909, pp. 46-57.

* 2. *Almanach d'architecture moderne*, Paris, G. Crès et Cie., pp. 139-166.

* 3. See Le Corbusier, *The Decorative Art of Today*, translated by James I. Dunnett, (originally published as *L'Art décoratif d'aujourd'hui*, Paris, Crès, 1925), London, Architectural Press, 1987.

* 4. *L'Hôtel du collectionneur*, preface by Léon Deshairs, Paris, Edtions Albert Lévy, 1926.

* 5. Jean Badovici, *L'Architecture vivante*, 1925.

* 6. Waldemar George, "L'Exposition des arts décoratifs de 1925. Les tendances générales", *L'Amour de l'Art*, 1925, pp. 285-286.

* 7. *L'Amour de l'Art*, 1925, p. 174.

* 8. Inquiry by René Chavance, *Art et Décoration*, January-June, 1922, p. 55.

1. The history of the exhibition is retraced in *Avis présenté au nom de la commission du Commerce et de l'Industrie sur le projet de loi concernant l'Exposition internationale des arts décoratifs et industriels modernes*, Chambre de Députés, session de 1923, n⁰ 5849, p. 2.

2. This was the first major "specialized" international exhibition held in France. After the Exposition universelle of 1900, the tradition of holding a universal exhibition every eleven years since 1855 was halted, mainly because they were considered too large and too expensive, and because of the increasing frequency with which they were being held throughout Europe and the United States, as pointed out in an enquiry held by the Ministry of Commerce in 1911. Archives Nationales, F12 8834.

3. Alain Beltran and Pascal Griset, *La croissance économique de la France 1815-1914*, Armand Colin, Paris, 1988, pp. 159-160.

4. Couyba was named an honorary member of the Société in 1910 for his support of the Société's efforts. In 1927, he was appointed director of the Ecole nationale des arts décoratifs. Charles M. Couyba, *Rap-*

port portant sur la fixation du budget général de l'exercice de 1907, Ministère de l'instruction publique, des Beaux-Arts et des Cultes, Paris, 1906.

5. See "De l'art social et de la nécessité d'en assurer le progrès par une exposition", *Idées Modernes*, vol. 1, January 1909, pp. 46-57. In 1913, the text was reprinted in book form along with reactions by the press and the artistic community under the title *L'Art Social*. Roger Marx (1859-1913) had been an avid supporter of the cause of the decorative arts in France. Born in Nancy, he was a friend and champion of the work of Emile Gallé. After his arrival in Paris, he was named Inspector of Provincial Museums, and continued his support of the applied arts by petitioning for an autonomous salon. For more on Roger Marx see Madeleine Rebérioux, "De l'art industriel à l'art social: Jean Jaurès et Roger Marx", *Gazette des Beaux Arts*, February, 1988, pp. 155-158, and Camille Morineau, *Roger Marx*, DEA, Université de Paris VIII, 1988.

6. *Procès-verbal du Comité de la Société des artistes décorateurs*, December 1910, p. 17.

7. René Guilleré, *Rapport sur une Exposition internationale des arts décoratifs modernes*, Paris 1915, Paris 1911, *Archives François Carnot*, bibliothèque des Arts décoratifs, Paris. The Société d'encouragement à l'art et à l'industrie was founded following the Exposition universelle of 1889 by Gustave-Roger Sandoz. Each year, the society awarded several prizes at the Salons of the Société.

8. Guilleré, pp. 3-4.

9. The *projet de loi* was submitted to the Chamber by François Carnot, Joseph Paul-Boncour, Henry Cochin, Marcel Sembat, Joseph Reinach. See typed manuscript *Archives Carnot*, bibliothèque des Arts décoratifs, Paris.

10. Ministère du Commerce et de l'Industrie, Commission préparatoire de l'Exposition internationale des arts décoratifs modernes, *Rapport de M. François Carnot, Deputé chargé de l'étude du programme*, 10 Decembre 1912.

11. Rapport Carnot, p. 4.

12. These issues are discussed in Alphonse Deville, *Rapport au nom de la 4e Commission sur les projets et pétitions relatifs à la date et au caractère de l'Exposition (proje-*

tée) des arts décoratifs et des industries d'art, Conseil Municipal de Paris, 1912.

13. For the economic situation in France in the 1920s see Richard F. Kuisel, *Capitalism and the State in Modern France*, Cambridge University Press, 1981, Chapter 3.

14. *Exposition internationale des arts décoratifs et industriels modernes, son objet, son programme, son importance économique*, Paris 1922, Archives Nationales F21 4075.

15. Arthur Levasseur, *Avis présenté au nom de la commission du commerce et de l'Industrie sur le projet de loi concernant l'Exposition internationale des arts décoratifs et industriels modernes*, Chambre de Députés, Session de 1923, n° 5849.

16. *Procès-verbal de l'assemblé générale de la Société des artistes décorateurs*, 8 March 1924.

17. "Pour l'Exposition de 1925, la part des décorateurs", *Le Bulletin de la vie artistique*, n° 6, 1925, pp. 11-12. It may be interesting to compare some of the subsidies requested from the Ministry of Fine Arts by several of the decorators for the execution of their contributions to the Ambassade. Jean Dunand requested 30,000 francs for the execution of four armchairs, four stools, one divan, and one table for his *Smoking-room* in black lacquer. Jacques-Emile Ruhlmann asked for 65,000 francs for the execution of one chest in amboyna wood. Pierre Chareau asked for 21,500 francs for one armchair and a desk for his *Office-Library*. Francis Jourdain requested 9,499 francs for four armchairs displayed in his *Smoking-room*. Archives nationales, F21 4075.

18. Gabrielle Rosenthal, "Le cour des Métiers et l'Ambassade française", *L'Art Vivant*, special edition, 1925, p. 22.

19. *Bulletin de la Vie Artistique*, 15 November 1925, p. 494.

20. Cited in Waldemar George, "L'Exposition des arts décoratifs et industriels de 1925, les tendances générales", *L'Amour de l'Art*, 1925, pp. 285-286.

21. E. Tériade, "Un an après, quelques considérations sur les arts décoratifs", *Les Arts de la maison*, Autumn, 1926.

1926-1929

*1. Léon Werth, "Le XVIIᵉ Salon des artistes décorateurs", *Art et Décoration*, January-June, 1927, pp. 162-163.

1. Unsigned article, "Mobiliers pour français moyens", *Bulletin de la vie artistique*, n° 7, January, 1926, p. 6.

2. Fernand David, "Préface", *Catalogue du XVIᵉ Salon de la Société des artistes décorateurs,*" 1926, pp. 1-2.

3. Yvanhoe Rambosson, "Le salon des artistes décorateurs", *La Revue de l'art ancien et moderne*, July-August, 1926, p. 96.

4. Rambosson, p. 94.

5. Ernest Tisserand, "Le XVIᵉ Salon des artistes décorateurs", *L'Art Vivant*, vol. 4, June 1926, p. 415. Tisserand continued his campaign criticizing the direction that the Société was taking in his review of the Salon of 1927, when he remarked: "We are in fact witnessing the rout of a certain kind of decorative art whose luxurious clichés are positively revolting to people today. The pontiffs of this type of art take the best places and spread themselves out. But they are very visible there and easy targets. And if critics do not yet dare to speak out openly, the public has no such qualms." Ernest Tisserand, "Le XVIIᵉ Salon des Artistes-Décorateurs", *L'Art Vivant*, June 1927, p. 414.

6. See Jean Porcher, "La maison nouvelle à l'étranger", *Art et Décoration*, vol. 52, 1927, pp. 183-192.

7. Jean Gallotti, "The Decorative Work of Djo-Bourgeois", *The Arts*, vol. 14, 1928, p. 164.

8. Jean Gallotti, "Le Salon des artistes décorateurs", *The Arts*, vol. 14, 1928, p. 23.

9. These discussions are recorded in *Procès-verbal de l'assemblée générale de la société des artistes décorateurs*, 27 February 1930.

10. Conversation with the author, March 1985.

11. Ernest Tisserand, "Chronique de l'art décoratif", *L'Art Vivant*, 1929, p. 372.

12. Except for Djo-Bourgeois, who rejoined the Société in 1930.

13. Conversation with the author.

14. Francis Jourdain, "Origin and Raison d'Etre of the New Society", *Creative Art*, vol. VII, July-December 1930, p. 369.

15. Louis Cheronnet, "La section française du XXe Salon des artistes décorateurs", *Art et Décoration*, July 1930, pp. 1-2.

16. Charles Hairon, "Avant-propos", *Bulletin de la Société des artistes décorateurs*, 15 March 1929, p. 2.

17. *Procès-verbal de l'assemblée générale de la société des artistes décorateurs*, 7 July 1928, p. 9. The specific event that provoked this change in policy was an exposition reserved for manufacturers, "La Décoration française contemporaine", that was to be held under the auspices of the Union centrale des arts décoratifs in January 1929.

18. *Procès verbal de l'Assemblé Générale de la Société des artistes décorateurs*, 26 June 1930, p. 20.

19. Yvanhoé Rambosson, "Le Salon des artistes décorateurs", *La Revue de l'art ancien et moderne*, vol. LVI, July-August, 1929, pp. 298 and 303.

20. André François-Poncet, "Une opinion ministérielle sur l'art décoratif moderne", *Les Echos d'art*, n° 54, January 1930, p. 28.

21. *Bulletin de la Société des artistes décorateurs*, 1 October 1926, p. 36.

22. Pierre Rameil, *Bulletin de la Société des artistes décorateurs*, 1 October 1926, p. 32.

23. Fernand David, "Preface", *Catalogue du XVIe Salon de la Société des artistes décorateurs*, 1926, p. 3.

24. Léon Werth, "Le XVIIe Salon des artistes décorateurs", *Art et Décoration*, 1927, pp. 162-163.

25. See Paul Brandt, "Le 18e Salon des artistes décorateurs", *Art et Industrie*, June 1928, pp. 25-26.

26. W.C., "Le Salon des artistes décorateurs", *Journal d'ameublement*, June 1928, reproduced in *Charlotte Perriand, un art de vivre*, Musée des arts décoratifs/Flammarion, Paris, 1985, p. 17.

1930

*1. *Charlotte Perriand, Un Art de vivre*, p. 17.

1. The most complete study on the German Werkbund is by Joan Campbell, *The German Werkbund: The Politics of Reform in the Applied Arts*, Princeton, 1978.

2. "Le Werkbund allemand au salon des artistes décorateurs", *Art et Décoration*, Chronique, March 1930, p. II.

3. Ibid, p. III.

4. *Catalogue de la section allemande, Exposition de la Société des artistes décorateurs*, Berlin, 1930.

5. *Bulletin de la Société des artistes décorateurs*, 15 February 1930, p. 11.

6. Pierre Lavedan, "Le Salon des décorateurs", *L'Architecture*, vol. XLIII, n° 7, 1930, p. 29.

7. Ibid, p. 229.

8. Ibid, p. 230.

9. Ibid, p. 236.

10. Marcel Zahar, "Le Salon des artistes décorateurs", *Art et Industrie*, n° 6, June 1930.

11. Gaston Varenne, "Le Vingtième Salon des artistes décorateurs et les problèmes de l'art moderne", *Die Forme*, vol. 5, 1930, p. 436.

12. Varenne, p. 436.

13. Varenne, p. 438.

14. Wilhelm Lotz, "Exposition der Deutscher Werkbund à Paris" *Die Form*, vol. 5, 1930, p. 292. It should be said here that the position of the Werkbund in 1930 was not as stable as Lotz would have had his readers believe. That year, Werkbund funds had been drastically cut, and growing nationalist factions within the organization were beginning to protest against its almost exclusive emphasis on functionalist design. See Campbell, pp. 207-242.

15. Lotz, p. 287.

16. "Hypermodernisme", *La Revue de l'art ancien et moderne*, July-August, 1930, p. 282.

1931-1942

1. For an analysis of the effects of the crisis of the 1930s on political and intellectual life in France see J.-L. Loubet del Bayle, *Les non-conformistes des années trente*, Editions du Seuil, Paris, 1969.

2. Lucie Holt Le Son, Louis Sognot, Jean Prouvé, Rose Adler, and Sonia Delaunay left to join the Union des artistes modernes. See *Procès-verbal de l'assemblée générale de la Société des artistes décorateurs*, 15 December 1930.

3. Paul Follot, "A nos camarades", *Bulletin de la Société des artistes décorateurs*, 15 November 1931.

4. In particular against the members of the Union des artistes modernes. See Suzanne Tise, "Manifeste 1934", in *Les Années UAM*, exhibition catalogue, musée des Arts décoratifs, Paris 1988.

5. Paul Iribe, "Profits et pertes", *Ameublement et Décoration*, 1931, pp. 5-7.

6. Paul Iribe, *Défense du luxe*, Draeger Frères, Paris, 1932.

7. See Arsène Alexandre, "Défense du luxe", *La Renaissance*, July-August, 1932.

8. It was to this that Le Corbusier replied in his *Croisade ou le Crépuscule des académies*, published in 1933. See Jean-Claude Vigato, "Croisade", in *Le Corbusier une encyclopédie*, éditions du Centre Georges Pompidou, Paris, 1987, p. 111. See also Jean-Claude Vigato, "Exposition et positions architectoniques", in *Cinquantenaire de l'exposition internationale des arts et techniques dans la vie moderne*, Institut français d'architecture/Paris Musées, 1987, pp. 336-347.

9. André Arbus, "Les besoins individuels et le meuble", *L'Encyclopédie française*, Vol. XVI, 1935, Chapter II, p. 5. Romy Golan has examined the effects of the Depression on painting in France during the 1930s and the return to agrarian values that many believed could preserve France from the economic ruin facing more industrialized nations. See *A Moralized Landscape: The Organic Image of France Between the Two World Wars*, Ph.D. dissertation, Courtauld Institute of Art, London, 1989.

10. The project was proposed for 1935 by Radical deputy Julien Durand, president of the Commission of Commerce. On the evolution of the exhibition project see

Jean-François Pinchon, "La conception et l'organisation de l'Exposition", in *Cinquantenaire de l'Exposition internationale*, Institut français d'architecture/Paris Musées, 1987, pp. 36-43.

11. Ibid, p. 36.

12. *Procès-verbal de l'assemblée générale de la Société des artistes décorateurs*, 18 June 1931, p. 44.

13. Their first meeting was held on 8 December 1931 at the Musée des arts décoratifs. *Procès-verbal de l'assemblée générale de la Société des artistes décorateurs*, 15 March 1932, p. 28.

14. *Procès-verbal de l'assemblée générale de la Société des artistes décorateurs*, 15 March 1932, p. 30.

15. *Procès-verbal du comité de la Société des artistes décorateurs*, 5 February 1934.

16. Pinchon, p. 37.

17. *Procès-verbal de l'assemblée générale de la Société des artistes décorateurs*, November, 1935, p. 5.

18. Maurice Barret left the Société after this to show with the Union des artistes modernes in the 1937 exhibition. *Procès-verbal de l'assemblée générale de la Société des artistes décorateurs*, 9 December 1935.

19. Anatole de Monzie, "Introduction", *Catalogue du pavillon de la Société des artistes décorateurs, Exposition internationale Paris-1937*. Anatole de Monzie served as Minister of Finance and then Minister of Public Education in 1925. He was Minister of National Education from 1932 to 1934.

20. Louis Cheronnet, "Intérieurs 1937", *Art et Décoration*, Vol. LXVI, 1937, pp. 257-258.

21. S. Gille-Delafon, "L'architecture au salon des artistes décorateurs", *Beaux-Arts*, 26 May 1939.

22. *Excelsior*, May 1939.

23. *Procès-verbal*, Assemblée générale de la Société des artistes décorateurs, 21 December 1931.

24. J. Hiriart, "Sur une image", *Catalogue du 22ᵉ Salon de la Société des Artistes Décorateurs*, 1932, p. 4.

25. Response by Waldemar George, "Evolution ou mort de l'ornement?" *Art et Décoration*, Les Echos d'art (supplement), June 1933, p. V.

26. Gaston Derys, "Le Vingt-troisième salon des artistes décorateurs", *Mobilier et Décoration*, 1933, pp. 203-204.

27. J.P. Sabatou, "Le 24ᵉ Salon des artistes décorateurs", *Architecture d'Aujourd'hui*, 1934, p. 78.

28. Maurice Barret, "Au Salon des artistes décorateurs, les uns s'attardent ou s'adaptent, d'autres trop peu nombreux prévoient . . . l'equipement rationnel de l'habitation", *Le Décor d'Aujourd'hui*, June 1935, pp. 26-27.

29. This trend was launched in a contemporary exhibition organized by Waldemar George entitled *Formes d'Aujourd'hui*, held in the Galerie Art et Industrie (28 April-18 May 1936). See article in *Art et Industrie*, April 1936.

30. The Salon de la Lumière was founded in Paris in 1933. The profession of "ingénieur-éclairagiste", who studied the artistic and scientific usages of natural and artificial lighting, developed in France during the early 1920s. See Bernard Barraqué, "L'Eclairagisme entre art et science, Jean Dourgnon (1901-1985)", in *L'Electricité et ses consommateurs*, Paris, Editions PUF, 1987.

31. "Introduction", Catalogue du XXIXᵉ Salon des artistes décorateurs, 1939.

Index of artists who exhibited at the Salons and in the Pavilions of the Société des artistes décorateurs between 1904 and 1942.

Proper names are not always written with the correct diacritical marks, these often being omitted in the Salon catalogues.
In 1930, the Deutscher Werkbund was invited to exhibit at the Société's Salon. The names of the participating artists are found in a separate list at the end of the index.
In 1940, the Salon of the Société des artistes décorateurs was held in conjunction with the Salon d'Automne and the Salon des Tuileries.
The names in bold print correspond to the artists cited in the text and are accompanied by the page numbers where they appear. Page numbers in italics refer to the pages where an artist's work is illustrated.

A

C

Chabal Claude 1934
Chabert-Dupont Alice 1921, 1922, 1923, 1924, 1925, 1926, 1927, 1928, 1929, 1930, 1931, 1932, 1933, 1934, 1935, 1936, 1937, 1938, 1939
Chabrier Emmanuel 1923
Chadel Jules 1907
Challou Jacques 1929, 1933
Chalon Louis 1904
Chalot Jeanne-Mélanie-Marie-Léontine 1919
Chambost Pol 1942
Chameaux Suzanne 1926
Champetier de Ribes André 1932
Champion Geneviève 1938
Champion Georges 1924, 1926, 1928, 1929
Champion Maurice 1942
Champrosay 1942
Champseix André 1939
Chanal Eugène-Louis 1911
Chanson André 1928
Chanteaud-Chabas Germaine 1942
Chantrel Renée 1933, 1934, 1936
Chapelle Suzanne 1942
Chappey Marcel (1927, 1928, 1929, 1933, 1936) 152
Chapus Albert 1927, 1930
Charavel et Mélendès 1931, 1935
Charbonnier Pierre 1922
Chareau Pierre (1922, 1923, 1924, 1925, 1926) 46, 52, *55*, 60, 62, 63, 82, *83*, 87, 104, *106*, *107*, *108*, 114, 126, 132, 133, 142
Charles Madeleine 1921
Charlier Charles-Henri 1912
Charmaison Raymond 1922
Charmoy Georges-Raphaël 1904
Charpentier Charles 1904
Charpentier Marcel 1922, 1923, 1933
Charpentier Maurice 1911
Chartier Lyda 1942
Chassaing Edouard 1920, 1923, 1924, 1925
Chassard Marcel 1942
Chauchet-Guilleré Charlotte (1910, 1911, 1912, 1913, 1914, 1919, 1920, 1921, 1922, 1923, 1924, 1937) 52, *59*, 74
Chaudière Pierre 1939
Chaumeil Henri 1920, 1933, 1934, 1935, 1936
Chauvaux Oscar 1932
Chauvel Marie-Blanche 1928, 1929, 1930, 1931, 1932, 1933, 1934, 1935, 1936, 1937, 1938, 1939, 1940, 1942
Chavannes Laure-Hélène 1914
Chedanne Georges 1911
Cheradame Jacques 1933, 1934, 1935
Cheron Georges 1928

Chevalier Fernand-Camille 1933
Chevalier Georges (1919, 1920, 1921, 1925, 1926, 1927, 1929, 1930, 1932, 1933, 1935, 1939, 1940, 1942) 87, *104*
Chevalier Robert 1926, 1929
Chevallier Louise-Edmée 1938, 1939, 1942
Chevrier Anne-Marie 1942
Chigot Francis 1910, 1911, 1912, 1913, 1914, 1919, 1920, 1921, 1922, 1923, 1924, 1925, 1926, 1928
Chmetz Théodore-André 1912, 1913, 1914
Chopard Gaston-Albert 1923, 1924, 1925, 1926, 1927, 1928, 1929, 1930, 1931, 1932, 1933, 1934, 1935, 1936
Christauflour Solange 1926
Christen André 1938
Ciechanowska Hélèna 1921
Cirulis Ausis 1911
Claude 1929
Claude P. 1919
Claude S.-Marguerite 1920
Claude Stéphane 1933
Claude-Levy Mlle 1927, 1928
Claude-Salvy Marie-Madeleine (1931, 1934, 1935, 1936, 1937, 1939) *237*, 239, 257, *258*
Claudet Georges-Max 1908, 1911
Clavel Jean-Robert 1936
Clément-Serveau 1928
Cless-Brothier Camille 1919, 1920, 1921, 1922, 1923, 1924
Clouzot Marianne 1928, 1942
Cochet Gérard 1922
Cochin Henry 1904
Cœffin Josette 1939
Cognet 1904
Cogneville Roger 1927, 1928, 1929
Coiffier Albert 1933
Colas Henri 1938, 1939, 1940, 1942
Colin Jean 1942
Colin Léo 1929
Colin Paul-Emile 1922, 1924
Colin Pierre 1928
Collet Edouard 1908, 1914, 1919, 1920, 1921, 1922, 1923, 1924, 1925
Collet Julien-Louis 1927
Collin André-Jules 1911, 1912, 1913
Collin Blanche-Marie-Anne 1906, 1912
Collinet Albert-Henri 1921
Collot André 1942
Colmant 1927, 1929
Colosiez Jean (1930) *167*, 171
Colotte Michel-Aristide 1927, 1930, 1931, 1932, 1933, 1938

Comminges Nahida de 1921
Constant Lucienne 1931
Contesse Gaston 1931, 1932, 1933, 1935, 1937
Conti Anita 1932, 1939
Contreau Julien-Louis 1920
Coquemer Léon 1942
Coquerel Claude 1932, 1934
Coquery René-Auguste 1919, 1920, 1922, 1923
Cordès Eva 1911
Cormier Joseph 1922
Cornebert Joseph 1931
Cornet 1942
Cornet Paul 1925
Cos-Tilhes Eugène 1904
Costa Joachim 1928, 1931
Costantin Hélène 1933, 1934
Couallier Robert-Philippe 1929, 1930
Coudyser 1906
Coudyser Jules 1908, 1910, 1911, 1912, 1913, 1914, 1919, 1920, 1921, 1922, 1923, 1924, 1926, 1927, 1928, 1929, 1930, 1931
Coudyser Mme 1911
Cougnet 1923
Coulier Henri 1907
Coupigny Mme Léo 1929
Courche François 1904
Courcoux Paul 1904, 1911
Courtray Victor 1942
Coutant Mlle 1925
Coutaud Lucien (1942) *242*
Couty Edme (1904, 1906, 1907) 18, 30, 31
Couyba Charlotte 1931
Coze Paul 1922
Cremier W.-André 1926
Crepy Marcelle 1942
Creston René 1936
Cretté Georges 1924, 1926, 1927, 1928, 1929, 1931, 1932, 1933, 1934, 1935, 1937, 1938, 1939, 1940, 1942
Creuzevault Henri-Albert 1929
Creuzevault Louis et Henri 1930
Crevel René 1921, 1922, 1923, 1925, 1927, 1929, 1930, 1934, 1936, 1940
Croix-Marie Paul 1904, 1907, 1908, 1910, 1911, 1912, 1913, 1914, 1919, 1920, 1921, 1936
Cronenfels Else de, dit Elsane 1932
Cros Louise-Henriette-Marcelle 1913, 1914, 1919
Cuny Louis 1927
Cuvelier-Dupuis Mme 1942
Cyriax Mlle Tony 1914

D

Dabault Henri-Ernest 1904
Dael Marie 1925
Dagot Louise-Amélie 1921, 1923
Daisay Alexandre 1922
Dalbet 1925
Dalbet Louis 1942
Dammouse Albert-Louis (1907, 1908, 1910, 1911, 1913) 18
Damon Robert-Jules-Georges 1932
Danjon Maurice-Louis 1932, 1933, 1934, 1936, 1938

Dariel Pierre 1921
Dariel-Favre Mme 1942
Dariel-Renard Fernand 1936
Dartigues Marie 1930
Daubner Marianne 1933, 1935
Daudet Lucien-Alphonse 1907
Daum Antonin 1921, 1923, 1924, 1925, 1928, 1926, 1930
Daum Paul 1927, 1931, 1933, 1934, 1935, 1936, 1937, 1942
Daurat Jacques 1933

Daurat Maurice (1912, 1920, 1921, 1922, 1923, 1924, 1925, 1926, 1928, 1929, 1930, 1931, 1932, 1933, 1934, 1935, 1936, 1937, 1938, 1939) 150, 181, *209*, *246*, 257
Davach de Thèze Marc 1938, 1939
David 1931
David Emile-Marcel 1926, 1927
David Fernand 1926
Davidoff Erna 1921
Davison G. D. 1914
Dayot Magdeleine 1912

Dupré Renée 1921, 1929, 1930
Duprez 1928
Dupuis Geneviève 1942
Durand Hélène 1928, 1929
Duret Marianne 1929, 1930
Duru Ernest-Edouard 1922

Duru Marguerite Emilie 1904
Dusouchet Pierre-Léon 1920
Dussour Louis-Félix-Aimé 1932, 1936
Dutfoy Germaine 1933
Duval Henri 1931
Duval Jean-Charles 1920, 1921, 1923

Duval Pierre 1936, 1938
Duvaux Georges 1932
Duvaux Jacques 1933
D'Yerna-Baud Albert-André 1936

E

Edelmann Charles-Auguste 1924, 1928, 1930, 1933
Edgar-Faure Lucie 1932, 1933, 1934, 1935, 1936, 1939, 1940
Edy Legrand Edouard 1936
Ehinger Jean 1914
Ekman Adrien 1933, 1935, 1942

Emerson Sybil 1931, 1932
Englinger Gabriel (1926, 1927, 1928, 1929, 1930, 1931, 1935, 1937) *123, 127, 135, 140, 180, 232, 244*
Eran Lise 1932, 1933
Ernest Yvonne 1933
Ernotte Jacques 1929

Espagnat Georges d' 1933, 1935, 1936
Estachy Françoise 1942
Eudes Marie 1933
Ewald Albert 1929
Expert Henri-Roger (1927, 1928, 1930) 150, 166, 181
Exter Alexandre 1942

F

Fabre Auguste-Victor 1924
Fache Jean et Jules 1920
Faguet Alexis Victor 1904
Falke Pierre 1922
Faraut Roger-Louis 1938
Farge Aline 1939
Farge Marie-Louise 1930
Fargue Léon 1922
Fau André 1926, 1929
Fau André et Guillard Marcel 1924, 1928
Faure Camille 1930
Faure François 1926
Faure Lucie-Edgar 1938
Faure Pauline 1912
Faureau Henri 1923
Faurè-Fremiet Blanche 1931, 1932
Favier Henri (1925, 1926, 1927, 1928, 1930, 1931, 1932, 1933, 1934, 1935, 1936) 150, 152, *190,* 244
Favrat Félicien 1934, 1936, 1939, 1942
Favre Auguste-Victor 1921, 1922, 1923
Favre Gisèle 1939
Favre Louis-Marie 1926, 1931
Favre Madeleine 1922
Favre-Pinsard Gisèle 1942
Favre-Stahly Claude 1938
Fayard Arthème 1942
Fayet Gustave 1923
Felice Marguerite de (1904, 1906, 1908, 1910, 1911, 1912, 1913, 1914, 1919, 1920, 1921, 1922, 1923, 1924, 1926, 1928, 1929, 1930, 1932) 68
Felix Robert-Emile 1933
Fenwick Ph. et Zentz d'Alnois 1931, 1932
Ferdegue Jean-Louis 1933
Ferenczy Noémi 1931
Fernand-Trochain Jean 1935
Fernandez Florencio 1935
Ferrand Gabrielle 1914

Ferrand Louis 1942
Feuillâtre Charles-Eugène 1919, 1922
Feuillâtre Eugène (1904, 1906, 1910, 1911, 1912, 1913, 1914, 1915, 1919) *24*
Feuillâtre Jean 1922
Feuillâtre Suzanne 1914
Feure Georges de 1914
Fiefer Albert 1938, 1939
Filschova Jindra 1912
Fischer Alice 1935, 1936
Fisker Kay 1930
Fix-Masseau Pierre 1942
Fjerdingstad Christian 1928, 1929, 1934, 1935, 1936
Flandrin Marthe 1942
Flandrin-Lattron 1942
Fleischer-Wiemans Max 1908
Fliasberg P. 1939
Florens Marguerite 1920
Floriane Mlle 1926, 1928, 1929, 1932, 1934, 1937
Fluchaire Octave 1913
Foley-Risler Amélie-Marie-Anne 1907
Follot Paul-Frédéric (1904, 1906, 1907, 1908, 1910, 1911, 1912, 1913, 1914, 1919, 1920, 1921, 1922, 1923, 1924, 1925, 1926, 1927, 1929, 1931, 1932, 1933, 1934, 1935, 1936, 1937) *14, 22, 26, 28, 30, 32,* 33, 34, 35, *41, 43,* 45, 46, *52, 69, 75, 76, 80, 82, 126, 143,* 244, *245,* 246
Fonseca Gaston de 1942
Fontaine Anne-Marie 1922, 1923, 1925, 1926, 1928
Fontaine Simonne 1937
Fontan Suzanne 1928
Fontayne René 1923, 1929, 1930, 1931, 1932, 1933, 1934, 1935, 1936, 1938, 1939, 1942
Forbin Maurice 1934
Foreau, Lex, Sonrel 1935, 1936

Forest 1931
Forestier Etienne 1933
Foucault 1925
Fougère Germaine 1923
Foujita Tsugouhara 1929
Founès Esther 1935
Fouque Marie-Rose 1942
Fouqueray Charles 1931
Fouquet Georges 1925
Fouquet Jean (1926, 1927, 1928) 131, 133
Fourgeaud Yvonne (1923, 1924, 1926, 1927) 146
Fourrier Géo 1930
Foy Roger 1922
Fraermann Théophile 1912
Francillon René 1913
Francis Paul 1931
Francisse Emile-Guy 1922
François Jean 1920, 1923
François Marc 1942
Franz Ostermann 1904
Fray Marguerite 1932, 1933, 1934, 1935, 1936, 1937, 1938
Fraysse Jean 1931
Frederic Maurice 1942
Fréchet André et Paul 1932, 1933, 1934, 1935
Fréchet André-Emile (1923, 1924, 1926, 1927, 1928, 1929, 1930, 1931, 1936, 1937) *50,* 60, 244, 246
Fréchet Annie 1921
Fréchet Ernest 1919
Fréchet Paul 1931, 1933, 1942
Frémond André 1912
Frémont Pierre 1929
Fressinet Jean 1932, 1933, 1934, 1935, 1936
Friedberger Serge 1931, 1932
Fromentier Paul 1942
Fuld Gertrude 1934

G

Gabriel René (1919, 1920, 1921, 1922, 1923, 1924, 1925, 1928, 1929, 1930, 1931, 1933, 1934, 1935, 1936, 1938) 124, *152, 168,* 169, *180, 201,* 203, 244, *245, 258*

Gagnon 1904
Gaillard Eugène (1907, 1908, 1910, 1911, 1912, 1913, 1914, 1919) *14, 31,* 32, 41, 66
Gaillard Pierre 1930, 1931, 1932, 1933

Galais-Phearault (ou Galais-Pheasant) Trado (ou Nado) 1929, 1930
Galatry Louis 1921
Galland Jacques 1920

H

Haas Lisette 1921, 1922, 1923, 1924, 1926
Habert Eugène 1904, 1906
Habert-Dys Jules-Auguste 1913
Haeffelin Marcel 1927
Haentgès Simon 1928, 1929, 1930, 1931, 1932
Hairon Charles-Edouard (1904, 1910, 1911, 1912, 1913, 1920, 1921, 1922, 1923, 1924, 1925, 1926, 1928, 1929, 1930, 1931, 1937) 41, 56, 58, 66, 73, 76, 80, 92, 133, 136, 137, 139, 142, 146, 150, 152, 181
Halbout Georges 1926, 1929
Hald Edouard 1931, 1935
Halley Charles-Louis 1932
Halou Alfred-Jean 1925, 1929
Halouze Edouard 1934
Hamanaka Katsu 1932, 1933, 1934, 1935, 1936, 1938
Hamm Henri 1906, 1907, 1919, 1921, 1923
Hanot Octave-Augustin 1919
Harang Raoul 1919, 1928
Hardel Jean-François 1934
Harders Carel 1919
Hartman Bertram 1924
Hastrel et Planchenault Mmes 1942
Havard et Queyrens 1929
Haviland Robert 1928
Haye-Valenciennes André 1942
Hebert-Coëffin Josette 1934, 1936
Heckly Louis-Clovis 1928, 1932, 1933, 1936
Heer William 1911, 1912, 1914
Hélie Marcel-Victor 1930, 1931, 1932
Hellé André 1925, 1930, 1931
Helu Henny-Lucie 1938
Hémard A.-Joseph 1919, 1922, 1923, 1928

Henches Valentine-Félicie-Elisabeth 1919, 1920, 1921, 1922, 1923, 1924, 1925, 1926
Hennequet E. 1928
Hennion Raphaël 1931, 1932
Henri Robert (1931, 1934) 244
Henriot Jules 1929, 1930
Henry Georges 1931, 1937
Henry Hélène (1925, 1928) 87, 110
Henry-Desire 1933
Hera Jean 1938
Herbst René (1922, 1923, 1924, 1926, 1928) 130, 131, 132, 133, 137, 146, *150*, 151
Herest Marie-Magdeleine 1942
Hérisson Nathalie Louise 1904
Hernandez Mateo 1920
Herpin André 1919
Hertenberger Fernand 1932, 1933, 1934
Hervé-Mathé Berthe-Marie 1910, 1912
Hervier Simone 1923
Hesse Jean 1935, 1936, 1937
Hétreau Rémy 1942
Hétreau Rémy et Jager Jeannine 1939
Heureux Andhrée d' 1904, 1906, 1907, 1911, 1912, 1914, 1921
Heurtebise Lucien Eugène Ollivier 1904
Heuvelmans Lucienne 1928, 1931, 1933
Heuvelmans Suzanne 1926, 1929, 1930
Heymann Marianne 1939
Higgins C.-O. 1934
Hilbert Georges 1938, 1939
Hiolle 1923
Hiriart Joseph (1928, 1934) 150, 244, 246, *249*, 252, 254
Hiriart Joseph, La-Faye F. et Lacourreye 1933

Hirtz Lucien 1906, 1907, 1911, 1922, 1928
Hissard Jeanne 1919
Hivert Marie-Thérèse 1936, 1937
Hofer André 1942
Hohermann Alice 1934
Holback-Chanal Alice 1904
Hollander Fernand 1932
Hollander Lucy 1931, 1933
Holt Le Son Lucie (1926, 1927, 1928, 1929) *130*, 146, *148*, 188
Hopkins Edna-Boies 1922
Hordynsky Georges 1931
Houber-Hollier Délide 1928
Houillon Louis 1904, 1906, 1908
Houriet Loys 1932
Hourriez Marc 1934, 1935, 1936, 1942
Hourriez Max-Georges 1933
Houseal Albert 1904
Huchard Henriette-Jeanne 1938, 1939
Hugo Jean 1925
Hugo Valentine 1942
Hugon Roland 1942
Huignard Henri-Emile 1934
Huillard Paul 1923
Humblot-Buirette Anna 1922
Hummel Thérèse 1923, 1924
Hunebelle André 1928, 1929, 1930
Huot Louisa Alexandrine Eugénie d' 1904, 1906, 1907, 1908
Hurault Charles 1942
Hure Marguerite 1929
Husson Henri 1910, 1911, 1912
Huzar Simone 1931

I

Icart L. 1928
Iche 1942
Imenitoff Nathan 1932

Ingrand Max (1934, 1935, 1936, 1937) 246, *247*
Ingrand Paule (1936, 1939, 1942) *225*, *247*
Inguimberty Joseph 1913, 1921

Iratchet Simone 1936, 1939
Iribe Paul (1932) 191, 192
Ivanoff-Vassilieff Vassil 1942

J

Jabeau Pierre 1942
Jacquemin André 1942
Jacques Ernest 1920
Jacques Lucien 1928
Jacques Rosa 1921
Jacquet Paul-Rémy 1920, 1921, 1922, 1923, 1924, 1926, 1927, 1932
Jacquin Georges-Arthur 1912, 1914
Jaéglé Georges 1926, 1929, 1930
Jallot Léon et Maurice (1929, 1931, 1933, 1934, 1936, 1937, 1938) 138, *245*
Jallot Léon (1906, 1907, 1908, 1910, 1911, 1912, 1914, 1920, 1921, 1923, 1924, 1925, 1926, 1927, 1928, 1930) *33*, *35*, 87, 98, *104*, 114, *137*, 146, 181
Jallot Maurice et Subes Raymond 1930
Jallot Maurice (1927, 1928, 1939, 1942) 249
Jamet-Baucour Berthe 1938

Janer Jeanne-Ernest 1935, 1937
Janin Suzanne 1928, 1931, 1932, 1933, 1934, 1935, 1936, 1942
Janniot Alfred (1924) 142, *144*
Janniot G. 1932, 1939
Janpeltier 1931
Jary Francis 1926, 1927, 1928, 1929, 1930, 1931, 1932, 1933, 1934, 1942
Jary François 1936, 1938
Jaulmes Gustave-Louis (1911, 1912, 1914, 1919, 1921, 1925, 1929, 1933, 1934, 1938) 97
Jaulmes Marie-G. 1919, 1923
Jeanès Jean-Ernest 1920, 1921, 1922, 1923, 1924, 1925
Jeanès Marilise 1925
Jean-Haffen Yvonne 1927, 1928, 1929, 1930, 1931, 1932, 1933, 1935, 1939, 1940
Jeanmaire Mme M. 1911

Jeanneret Rose-Baucis 1920
Jeannin Gaëtan (1925) 146, *148*
Jeannin Georges 1904
Jegon Jean 1942
Jensen Georg 1910, 1914, 1920, 1921, 1922, 1923, 1928, 1930, 1934, 1936
Jenson Edmond-Louis 1922
Joannon Etienne 1904
Joannon Jacques 1930
Join-Lambert Octave 1912
Jolivet 1904
Jolly André 1910, 1911, 1912, 1914, 1921
Jolly Fanny 1934
Jolly Marie-Madeleine 1934
Jorrand Antoine 1911, 1913
Jose-Martin 1927
Josset Raoul 1926
Jou Louis 1922

Rausch Constantin 1932
Ravo René 1942
Ray Joseph-Jean-Kef 1922, 1923, 1924, 1928, 1930, 1931, 1932, 1934, 1937
Raymond-Kœnig Jules 1929
Raymond-Nicolas Paul-Emile 1928
Rayvan-Canaux Germaine-Marie-Amélie 1923
Reboussin Roger 1934
Recoux Charles-Albert 1923
Reculon Joanny 1910, 1913, 1914, 1919, 1920, 1921, 1923, 1924
Redard 1925
Redard Henry 1933, 1934
Rees Adya van 1936
Regard Marie-Marguerite 1942
Regelsperger Georges-Louis-Martial 1920
Régent Louis-Pascal 1927, 1929
Régius 1904, 1906
Regnoul (-Barre) Suzanne 1933, 1934, 1935, 1936, 1938, 1942
Reinach Louis 1923, 1924
Remillier Jean-Paul 1932, 1933, 1934, 1935
Remon P.-H. et fils 1920
Renard Claude 1920
Renard Marcel 1924, 1925, 1926, 1928, 1929, 1930, 1934, 1935, 1936
Renato René 1929
Renaudot Lucie (1923, 1925, 1926, 1927, 1928, 1929, 1931, 1932, 1933, 1935, 1936, 1937) *79*, 181, 249
Renault Georges-René 1923
Renefer Raymond 1923, 1928, 1931
Renesson Rose 1935
René-Robert 1934, 1935, 1937, 1942
Reno Irène 1932
Renouvin Georges 1932
Repelin Colette et Germaine 1921
Revai Eva 1927, 1929
Revil Geneviève 1942
Revilliod-Grenaut Louise 1912, 1913, 1914, 1919, 1920
Reyllawal Georges 1919, 1920, 1921
Reymond Carlos 1920, 1921
Ribvière Pauline 1911, 1912, 1913, 1914, 1919, 1920, 1921
Ricci Virgile 1935
Richard Paul 1907, 1923
Richet Gaston 1913, 1920, 1927, 1940

Richon Paulette 1921, 1923, 1938, 1939
Riedberger Jacques-Henri 1936
Rieffel (-Anossoff) Arlette 1928, 1930
Riesterer Maurice 1936, 1937
Rigal Louis 1926
Rigaud Henri 1908, 1910
Riggenback Catinka 1929
Rij-Rousseau Jeanne 1926
Ringuet Ghislain-Jean-Alfred 1926, 1927
Rinuy André 1929
Rion Lucien-Ange 1922, 1930
Ripa de RoveredoYvonne 1911, 1924
Rischmann Gaston 1929, 1931, 1932
Risler & Carré 1911
Rispal Gabriel 1942
Rivaud André 1926, 1927, 1928, 1929, 1931
Rivaud Charles 1908, 1910, 1911, 1912, 1913, 1914, 1919, 1920
Rivière Pauline 1910, 1928
Rivir Armand 1924, 1925, 1926, 1929, 1942
Robert Anne 1928, 1929
Robert Eloi 1932
Robert Emile 1912, 1913, 1914, 1920
Robert Michel 1934
Robert René 1922, 1923, 1936, 1939
Roberts Jack 1921, 1931
Robichon Jean 1928
Robida Frédéric 1911, 1912, 1913
Robineau Adélaïde 1912
Robion Marguerite 1936, 1937
Roblin Marie 1910
Roche Camille-Auguste 1923, 1924, 1925, 1927, 1928, 1931, 1932, 1933, 1934, 1935, 1936, 1937, 1938, 1942
Roche Pierre (1904, 1906, 1907, 1908, 1910, 1911, 1912, 1903, 1919, 1920) 18
Roche Serge 1935
Rochier Louis 1938, 1939
Rodanet Henri 1938
Rodhain Dicta 1904
Rodier Jacques 1932, 1934, 1935
Rodier Jacques et Henri 1931
Rœ d'Albret et Siegriot 1927
Roger Emmanuel 1924, 1925
Rohde Johan 1928, 1930, 1933, 1936
Roig Pablo 1912
Roland-Gosselin Marie 1926, 1927
Rolland Berthe 1932

Rollet Hélène 1914
Rollin Lucien-Paul (1928, 1929, 1930, 1931, 1932, 1933, 1934, 1935, 1937) *152, 201, 232, 246, 247, 253*
Rollince Jeanne 1904, 1906, 1907, 1908
Romane Georges et André 1929
Romant Georges 1924, 1925, 1926, 1927, 1928, 1929, 1930, 1931, 1932, 1933, 1934, 1936
Romme Marthe 1919, 1920
Roques François 1923, 1926, 1927, 1928, 1929, 1930, 1931, 1932
Roquin Robert 1920, 1923, 1924
Rosbo Jean de 1942
Roscitano Ezio 1932
Rosenberg Kurt-Erman 1932
Rossi Francis 1927
Rostan Geneviève 1924
Rothschild Jean-Maurice 1933, 1934, 1935, 1936, 1939
Roulier Yvonne 1934, 1935, 1936
Rousseau Clément 1921
Roussy (-Louis) Suzanne 1919, 1920, 1921, 1922, 1923, 1924, 1925, 1926, 1927, 1942
Roux Gilberte 1932
Roux-Champion Victor-Joseph 1913, 1914, 1924
Roux-Colas Anne-Marie 1942
Roux-Spitz Michel (1923, 1924, 1925, 1926, 1927, 1928, 1929, 1930, 1932) *95, 125, 139*, 142, *167*, 169
Rovinsky Serge 1933, 1934, 1935, 1937, 1938, 1939, 1942
Roy Robert 1928, 1929, 1931, 1932
Royère Jean (1935, 1936, 1937, 1938, 1939, 1942) 239, *240*
Rual Jorj 1942
Rudier Eugène 1904
Ruelle Georges 1921, 1926
Ruepp Robert 1904, 1907
Ruhlmann Jacques-Emile (1911, 1919, 1920, 1921, 1922, 1923, 1924, 1925, 1926, 1928, 1929, 1930, 1932, 1933, 1934) 45, 62, 67, 73, *80*, 82, 83, 86, 112, *140*, 142, *144, 152*, 166, 181, *182, 192, 196*, 213, 246
Rumèbe Fernand 1911, 1913, 1914, 1919, 1920, 1921, 1922, 1923, 1924, 1925, 1942
Rutté Paul de 1923, 1932, 1933

S

Sabatier Suzanne 1931
Sabbagh Agnès 1919
Sabbagh Georges-H. 1919
Sabino Marius 1926, 1928, 1929, 1933, 1942
Saddier Fernand et Gaston 1926, 1928, 1931
Saglier François-Marcel 1934, 1935, 1938, 1939, 1942
Sainsère (-Lami) Christiane 1929, 1931, 1932, 1935,
Saint-André 1922, 1923, 1924
Saint-Cyr Jeannine de 1920
Saint-Georges Gaston 1919
Saint-Georges Jean 1925, 1939
Saint-Germain Marguerite de 1926, 1928, 1929

Saint-Gilles Jean 1931, 1932
Saint-Saëns Marc 1936, 1938, 1939
Sala Jean 1921, 1922, 1926, 1927, 1928, 1929, 1930, 1931, 1932, 1934, 1935, 1939, 1942
Salomon André (1939) 239, 260
Salomon Antony 1930
Sandier Alexandre 1906
Sandoz Edouard-Marcel 1911, 1913, 1914, 1919, 1920, 1921, 1922, 1923, 1924, 1926, 1927, 1928, 1931, 1932, 1936, 1942
Sandoz Gérard-Roger-Paul (1923, 1924, 1925, 1927, 1928) 131, 133
Sant'Andrea et Marceron 1923
Santin Hélène 1920

Sarlandie Jules 1910, 1926, 1930
Sarlandie Robert 1930, 1932
Saupique Georges 1925, 1926
Sauvage Henri et **Sarazin Charles** (1904) 18, *19*, 21, 30
Sauvage Marcel 1931
Sauvage Sylvain 1930, 1932, 1942
Savignac Raymond 1942
Savin Maurice 1939, 1942
Savina Joseph 1936
Savine Léopold 1904, 1916
Schaller-Mouillot Charlotte 1921, 1927
Scheidecker Franck (1904, 1906, 1907, 1908, 1910, 1911, 1913, 1914) 30

T

Thireau Lucile-Anna 1927
Thirion Claire 1931
Thiriot Pierre 1930, 1931, 1932
Thomas 1924
Thomas Auguste-Henri 1913, 1914, 1920, 1921, 1922, 1924
Thomas Hendrik 1933, 1935
Thomas Jean-François 1926
Thomas Lucien-Henri 1932, 1933, 1934
Thomas Monique 1935
Thomasson Donat 1931, 1932
Thorsson Nils 1932
Thos 1912
Tinota 1920
Tirefort Jean 1928, 1929, 1931, 1932, 1933
Tirefort Jean 1938
Tirman Henriette 1931
Tissier Léon 1911, 1912

Tissot Alfred 1925
Tita Terrisse 1939, 1942
Tolmer Alfred 1942
Tolmer Claude 1942
Touchagues Louis (1942) 260
Touchet Jacques 1929, 1931, 1933, 1935
Toulgouat Pierre 1928
Tourasse Georges 1932, 1935
Tourasse Jean 1932, 1933, 1934, 1936
Tournon Paul (1939) 260
Tourrette Etienne 1906, 1910, 1911, 1913, 1923
Tourte Suzanne 1935
Tourtin Henri et Plattier Henry 1934
Tœfferd François 1942
Tran Binh Loc 1934
Tranchant Maurice 1930, 1931, 1932, 1933, 1935, 1942
Traverse Pierre 1926, 1927, 1928, 1929, 1930,

1931
Traz Marie de 1921
Tribondeau George-Charles 1933, 1934, 1935, 1936, 1937, 1938
Tribout Georges (1921, 1928, 1934, 1936) 150
Tribout Jean 1935
Tribout-Jean Mme 1932
Tripet-Nizery Hélène-Marie 1920, 1921
Tronquet Jean-Raymond 1942
Truel Lucha 1936
Truelle Madeleine 1942
Truffier Adolphe Armand 1904, 1906, 1907, 1908, 1910, 1921, 1925, 1926, 1927, 1928, 1929, 1930, 1931, 1932
Tschumi Jean 1932, 1933
Tschumi Jean et Vermeil Henri 1934, 1935
Turck Georges 1907

V

Valabreque Eliane 1920, 1921
Valance Robert 1933, 1934, 1935, 1938
Valette Henri 1923
Vallgren Antoinette 1907, 1908
Vallgren Villé 1907, 1908
Vallombreuse Henri de 1904, 1907
Varbanesco Dimitri 1934
Vasarins V. 1928
Vasseur et Guilly 1937
Vassilieff Marie 1931
Vautier Renée 1935
Vautrin Line 1939, 1942
Venini 1934
Vera Paul (1911, 1920, 1921, 1922, 1927, 1928, 1933, 1934, 1938) 52, *55*
Verdier André 1932
Vergne Berthe 1919, 1921, 1922, 1923
Verly Robert 1933

Verneuil Viviane 1931, 1932
Vernier Emile-Séraphin (1906, 1907, 1910, 1911, 1925) 31, 49
Vernon Frédéric 1906, 1907
Verschneider Jean 1926
Vertès Marcel 1929, 1930
Veunevot et Cera R. 1927
Veronese 1933, 1939
Vial Mlle 1904
Vibert Jacques 1935
Vibert Max (1938, 1939) *210*
Vibert Mlle Max 1926, 1927, 1928, 1929, 1930, 1931, 1932, 1933, 1934, 1935
Vidalin Pierre et Alazard Jules 1931
Vignaud-Linossier Jeanne 1935
Vigneau Jean-André (1924, 1930) 260
Vigoureux Pierre 1926
Villemot Bernard 1942

Vilmorin Mme Philippe de 1931
Vimal Fernande 1922
Vionnet Madeleine 1922
Visinand Jeanne 1932
Vitry Louise 1929, 1931, 1932
Vof Maximilien 1922
Vogel Lucien 1919 ou 1921
Voguet 1925, 1931
Voguet Léon et Legrand Edy 1926
Voros Béla 1938
Voruz Elise 1904
Vovos Béla 1927, 1928, 1929
Vox Maximilien 1942
Vu-Gia 1942
Vucao Dam 1934
Vuilleumier Jean -L. 1930, 1931, 1932, 1933, 1934, 1935
Vuitton Gaston-Louis 1924, 1926, 1927, 1928

W

Wahart Louise Hélène 1928, 1929
Wahl Marcelle 1920, 1921, 1922, 1923, 1924, 1925, 1926, 1927
Waidmann Pierre 1904
Walcheren Christine van der Meer de 1912
Waldraff Frantz (1910, 1911, 1912, 1913, 1914) *38*
Wallet-Josse Blanche 1912, 1919
Walter Amalrie 1921
Walz Victor 1904

Warnet Henri 1927, 1928, 1929
Waroquier Henri de (1907, 1908, 1910, 1911, 1912, 1913, 1914, 1919, 1920, 1921) 33, 34
Wegener Gerda 1919
Wegerif-Gravestein Agathe 1910
Weil Myriem 1936
Weil Paulette 1931, 1932, 1934, 1936
Wery Emile 1923
Wesselhœft Mary 1910
Wild Evelyn 1926, 1928

Willig René 1921
Windels Fernand 1932
Wivdenko Olga 1934, 1936
Wlerick Robert 1923, 1924, 1925, 1926, 1931, 1932
Wuilleumier Jean-L. 1935
Wuilleumier Willy 1924, 1932, 1933, 1934, 1935, 1936, 1937, 1938, 1939
Wuster Charles Léopold 1904
Wyld Evelyn 1927, 1929, 1932

Y Z

Yencesse Hubert 1939
Ylen Jean-Paul d' 1932
Ysel Onslow Isabelle Maïde 1904
Yung Pierre 1921
Zachary Margot 1932, 1933
Zack Léon 1929
Zadkine Ossip 1928, 1930

Zarraga Angel 1932, 1933, 1939
Zendel Joseph 1927, 1928
Zenker Paul 1922
Zénobel Pierre 1928, 1929, 1931, 1934
Zervudaki Lina 1933, 1934, 1935, 1936, 1938, 1939
Zillhardt Madeleine 1919

Zingg Jules-Emile 1919, 1920, 1921, 1922, 1935
Zinoview Alexandre 1921, 1923, 1924
Zipélius et Brillouin Mlles 1936, 1938, 1939, 1942
Zipélius Jeanne 1923, 1934, 1935
Zola Liberato 1914
Zuidel Joseph 1926

Salon de 1930 : Artists showing
in the German section presented
by the Deutscher Werkbund and organized
by Walter Gropius

B

Baake Hans
Baer Kurt
Bartning Otto
Bayer Herbert 160, 161, 162, *163, 179*
Berthold Heinrich
Beyer Lis
Bloedner August
Blum Eduard
Brandt Marianne
Breuer Marcel 127, 160, *162, 163, 179*
Bruehlmann Nina
Brugger Otto
Burchartz Max

D

Dell Christian
Dieker Friedel
Dœcker Richard

F

Feininger Lux
Finsler Walter

G

Glueckauf Karl
Gropius Walter *160, 161, 171, 181*

H

Habermann Erica
Hablik Lindemann
Haesler Otto
Hammesfahr Gottlieb
Hartwig Josef
Hennig Pr
Herman Alex
Herre Richard
Herrmann Louis
Hillerbrand Joseph
Holzinger Ernst
Horn Hilde
Huegel Elfriede von

J

Jacobi

K

Koenig Lutz
Konwiarz Richard
Kramer Ferdinand
Krumm Ludwig
Kuppenheim Ernst

L

Lahmann Alice
Landwehr Fritz
Lang Georg
Lauer Georg
Lettre Ella
Lindstroem Carl
Link Franz
Lorch Tilli

M

Manz Lorenz
Marcus Paul
Mauder Pr
May Ernst
Mendelsohn Erich
Mendelsshon von Stoessl Eva
Mies van der Rohe Ludwig
Moholy Lucia
Moholy-Nagy Ladislaus 160, 161, 162

N

Naumann Margarete
Nitschke Walter

P

Peterhans Walter
Petschow Robert

R

Rancke Ernst

Riebicke G
Ritter-Kaufmann Irmgard
Rittweger Otto

S

Schaefer C.R.
Scharoun Hans
Schlemmer Oscar
Schneck Adolf G. *179*
Schub-Semestrey Dr Berta
Schumacher Hans
Schweitzer O.E.
Seeger Karl
Seifert Curt
Sluzky Naum
Soellner Hans
Steiff Margarete
Stern Ernst
Stone Sasha
Straus Paula

T

Taut Bruno
Taut Max
Thomee Albert
Tuempel Wolfgang
Treskow Elisabeth

V

Vogt Hans
Vorhoelzer

W

Wagenfeld Wilhelm
Weech S. von
Wenz-Vietor Else
Wersin Wolgang von
Weyersberg Gottfried-Soehne
Winde Th. A.
Wingen Anton
Wolf Joseph

Z

Zimmermann Christian

Acknowledgements_____

Except for the records of the committee meetings and General Assemblies, the Société des artistes décorateurs possesses few archives on the period 1901-1942. Through the generosity and enthusiasm of two of our members, Etienne-Henri Martin and Maxime Old, however, we were able to reassemble much of the photographic documentation. We are also indebted to Mrs. Gascoin, Mrs. Gorse, Mrs. Kohlmann, Ms. G. Martineau-Dausset, Mr. J. Dumond, Mr. B. Dunand, Mr. B. Durussel, Mr. George Goetz, Mr. M. Mortier, Mr. J. Rothschild, and above all, to our colleagues who have passed away during these three years of research: Paul Beucher, André Preston, Gilbert Poillerat, and Maurice Pré.

Jean-Pierre Khalifa

We owe a special debt to the following for their patient and generous assistance:
Mrs. F. Adnet, Mrs. Y. Amic (bibliothèque des Arts décoratifs, Paris), Ms. R. Bargiel (musée de la Publicité, Paris), Ms. M. de Beyrie (galerie Maria de Beyrie), Mr. A. Blondel, Ms. G. Bonté (bibliothèque des Arts décoratifs, Paris), Mr. C. Boutonnet (galerie L'Arc-en-Seine), Mr. G. Bramy (galerie Bramy), Mr. Brugnot (galerie Brugnot), Mr. G. Bugeon, Ms. F. Camard, Mr. J.-P. Camard, Ms. L. de Caune, Ms. Cheska (galerie Vallois), Ms. D. Clemenceau (Fondation Vuitton), Mr. T. Couvrat-Desvergnes (galerie Couvrat-Desvergnes), Ms. S. Day (Institut français d'architecture), Ms. G. Delaporte (Curator at the musée des Arts décoratifs, Paris), Ms. E. Delecourt (Sygma-Illustration), Mrs. Dufet-Bourdelle, Mr. F. Duret-Robert, Mr. J.-J. Dutko (galerie Dutko), Ms. S. Edard (Photographic Service of the musée des Arts décoratifs), Ms. M.-N. de Gary (Curator at the musée des Arts décoratifs, Paris), Ms. N. Gasc (Curator at the musée des Arts décoratifs, Paris), Mr. Y. Gastou (galerie Yves Gastou), Ms. V. Humbert (musée de la Publicité), Mr. Jutheau, Mr. Kieger (galerie Suger), Mr. P. Kjellberg, Mr. G. Landrot (galerie Landrot), Ms. D. Le Cesne, Mr. A. Lesieutre, Ms. Magnan (galerie Makassar), Mr. A. Manoukian, Mr. F. Marcilhac (galerie Marcilhac), Mr. Maubaris (Studio Siégel et Stockmann), Mr. M. Mazet (galerie Suger), Ms. Millecamps, Mr. J. Nestgen, Mr. J.-L. Olivié (Curator at the musée des Arts décoratifs, Paris), Mr. R. Ortiz (galerie L'Arc-en-Seine), Ms. C. Perriand, Mr. Raid-Perzel (Ateliers Jean Perzel), Mr. E. Philippe (galerie Philippe), Ms. C. Plossu (Georg Jensen), Ms. Poillerat, Ms. E. Possémé (Curator at the musée des Arts décoratifs, Paris), Mr. Poulain, Mr. L. Rollin, Ms. M. Ruby (Collections Albert Kahn), Ms. J. Sartre (bibliothèque des Arts décoratifs, Paris), Mr. M. Souillac, Mr. J. de Vos (galerie de Vos).

Yvonne Brunhammer et Suzanne Tise

Photographic Acknowledgements⎯⎯⎯⎯⎯

Bibliothèque des Arts décoratifs, Paris 3, 4, 7, 8, 10, 17, 18, 46, 48, 49, 58, 64, 105, 106, 149, 151, 167, 178, 179, 181, 191, 192, 193, 194, 195, 196, 197, 200, 203, 207, 216, 218, 221, 227, 229, 243, 258, 276, 284, 286, 288, 294, 295, 296, 316, 323, 330; bibliothèque des Arts décoratifs, Paris, Collection Maciet 19; Florence Camard 78, 154, 164, 169, 232; studio Chevojon/SPADEM 148, 163; Jean Collas 190, 326; Philippe R. Doumic 144, 170; Mrs. Dufet-Bourdelle 209, 210, 252; Flammarion 2, 6, 21, 42, 50, 53, 54, 59, 65, 66, 76, 81, 102, 152, 153, 156, 183, 214, 217, 231, 240, 244, 245, 271, 282, 291, 297, 307, 308, 311; galerie Félix Marcilhac 16, 155; galerie L'Arc-en-Seine 100, 158, 211, 270, 309; Institut français d'architecture, Étienne Kohlmann archives 172, 199, 215, 226, 264; Institut français d'architecture, Louis Süe archives 272, 273, 274, 275, 277, 278, 279, 280, 281, 285, 287, 329; Collections Albert Kahn 110, 111, 116, 137, 138, 141; musée de la Publicité 1, 33, 39, 43, 87, 107, 113, 171, 251, 256, 283; musée des Arts décoratifs 120, 124, 129, 136, 139, 140, 143, 145; musée des Arts décoratifs, Louis Sognot archives 225; musée des Arts décoratifs, Editions Albert Lévy 108, 109, 112, 114, 142, 150, 159, 166, 173, 174, 175, 176, 177, 230, 234, 236, 298, 299, 302, 303, 304, 305, 306, 310; musée des Arts décoratifs, Sully-Jaulmes: 11, 20, 25, 30, 31, 32, 41, 70, 74, 94, 95, 160, 198, 228, 238; Maxime Old archives 260, 328; Jean Perzel: 126, 202, 315; Réunion des musées nationaux 9, 15, 29, 37, 38, 44, 45, 55; cristalleries Saint-Louis 51; Archives of the Société des artistes décorateurs: 12, 13, 14, 22, 23, 24, 26, 27, 28, 34, 35, 36, 40, 47, 56, 57, 60, 61, 62, 63, 67, 68, 69, 71, 72, 73, 75, 77, 79, 82, 83, 84, 85, 86, 88, 89, 90, 91, 93, 96, 97, 98, 99, 101, 103, 104, 115, 117, 118, 119, 122, 123, 125, 127, 128, 131, 132, 133, 134, 135, 146, 147, 157, 161, 162, 165, 182, 184, 185, 187, 188, 189, 201, 204, 205, 206, 208, 212, 213, 219, 220, 222, 233, 235, 237, 239, 241, 246, 248, 257, 259, 262, 263, 265, 266, 267, 268, 289, 290, 292, 293, 300, 301, 312, 313, 314, 317, 319, 320, 321, 322, 324, 325, 327, 331, 332; Sygma-Illustration 121, 186, 223, 242, 247, 249, 250, 254, 261, 269, 318; Suzanne Tise 168, 180, 253; H. Roger-Viollet 224; Harlingue-Viollet 130; N.D. Roger-Viollet 5, 255.